# LONDON TRANSPORT
## *in the 1930s*

Michael H. C. Baker

Ian Allan PUBLISHING

# Contents

First published 2007

ISBN (10) 0 7110 3131 2

ISBN (13) 978 0 7110 3131 9

Published by Ian Allan Publishing

an imprint of Ian Allan Publishing Ltd, Hersham, Surrey, KT12 4RG

Printed in England by Ian Allan Printing Ltd, Hersham, Surrey, KT12 4RG

Code: 0705/A3

Visit the Ian Allan Publishing website at www.ianallanpublishing.com

# Introduction

No 40, a former South Metropolitan Electric Tramways car built by Brush in 1906, stands at the West Croydon terminus of the Crystal Palace route in February 1936. This archaic vehicle would be replaced a few days later by an almost-silent, smooth-running, state-of-the-art trolleybus. *E. G. P. Masterman*

D ID the motor bus ever make such strides in comfort, technical specification and performance as in the years between 1930 and 1940? As this is a rhetorical question I shall, dear reader, provide an instant answer, which is 'No'. And nowhere was this more obvious than in London. When the decade opened some bus journeys would have been in vehicles with solid tyres, many double-deckers had no upper-deck roofs, and practically all would have brackets, pillars and various protruding fitments seemingly designed to catch unwary passengers in various painful parts of their anatomy as they lurched and bumped over what, in places, were far-from-smooth road surfaces. Most passengers would still have been pretty content with all this, having in their younger days been accustomed to horse-drawn modes of transport.

The tramcar was still the standard conveyance for many Londoners. No fewer than 423 trams passed along the Embankment within sight of the Houses of Parliament every hour during peak periods. Most cars, but not all, did have upper-deck roofs, although the seats were probably not upholstered, and the driver would be exposed to everything the weather and the often dirty streets — for there were still tens of thousands of horses at work — could throw at him. But many of the trams, particularly those belonging to certain boroughs, were old-fashioned and worn-out, and even the standard LCC car dated back the best part of 30 years to before World War 1. Revolutionary designs were just over the horizon, but the tram was essentially seen as out of date, an archaic means of transport holding up the march of the internal combustion engine.

Probably the most comfortable form of public transport was the Underground train, particularly on the District and Metropolitan lines, although the fact that it was possible to rattle below London's streets with the doors wide open was somewhat disconcerting. Deeper down, in the 'Tube', the ride was distinctly lively, and not all of each carriage was available to passengers, technology not yet having reached the point where everything electrical and mechanical could be stowed away beneath the floor.

Out in the furthest suburbs, in 'Metro-land' and the rural Home Counties, the scene was highly

*Above left:* A Fox cameraman films the burning of withdrawn K-type buses in the grounds of Alexandra Palace in 1930. *London's Transport Museum*

*Below left:* Hyde Park Corner in 1937. A policeman holds up a collection of taxis, saloon cars, a van and a lorry to allow two standard STLs and various other vehicles to make their way westwards. *London Transport*

*Above:* ST409 and NS2236 stand on Crystal Palace Parade in 1931. Despite its covered top the NS retained solid tyres, emphasising the advance in design represented by the ST. This location is still much used as a bus terminus, although Paxton's magnificent Crystal Palace, relic of the Great Exhibition of 1851, was to burn down on the night of 30/31 November 1936. *The Omnibus Society*

varied, with a host of operators, large and small, providing services with a huge mixture of vehicles, some of them very small with fewer than 20 seats, designed to penetrate the rural vastness down often-unmade country lanes. Car ownership was still very much for the more affluent, male-dominated middle and upper classes, and nearly everyone was dependent upon public transport for both getting to work and pleasure trips.

The Green Line network as such did not officially come into being until 1930, but a number of express services from the outer suburbs and beyond were already in existence. These were, in the main, worked by much the most comfortable of public-service vehicles, almost luxurious, fitted with handsome interiors, well-upholstered seats and mounted on the latest AEC Regal and Leyland Tiger chassis. At weekends vast numbers of Londoners travelled out into the country, to Epping Forest, the Surrey and Chiltern hills, historic towns such as Tunbridge Wells, Westerham, Windsor, St Albans, Guildford, and many routes from Central London and the inner suburbs were extended on Saturdays and Sundays to cater for this traffic. On Saturdays the exodus would not begin until early afternoon, most people working Saturday mornings.

The London General Omnibus Co, the London County Council and the Underground Electric Railway Co, collectively known as the Combine, were

*Left:* An Edward McKnight Kauffer poster of 1929 for the LGOC, featuring one of the Central London routes which penetrated deep into the Home Counties countryside. *London's Transport Museum*

*Right:* Streamlining reaches its apotheosis. One of the remarkable-looking, streamlined 'Tube' trains of 1935. *London's Transport Museum*

*Below right:* London Transport took the welfare of its staff and their families seriously. An egg-and-spoon race approaches a nail-biting finish at a Chiswick sports day in 1938. *London's Transport Museum*

far and away the biggest providers of public transport in and around London. There were also no fewer than 54 bus companies that were totally independent of any of the Combine, but although they operated a fascinating collection of vehicles and have attracted much historical interest they were actually of little significance, providing a mere 6% of services within the Metropolitan area.

Rather bigger players, taken together, were the tram networks of the municipalities. Some 20 or more years earlier, at the dawn of the new century, it had been virtually a matter of pride for a town which considered itself of any importance to emphasise its forward-looking attitude by providing electric trams for its citizens. They did not come cheap, track-laying being not only disruptive of other traffic but also expensive, as was all the necessary ancillary equipment, but many authorities considered it worthwhile. However, once the system was up and running it was usually highly efficient and popular and made a profit that could be ploughed back to subsidise the rates.

Having been born in 1937 I cannot claim an intimate first-hand experience of the decade, although I do have a distinct memory of a coach trip to Broadstairs in the summer of 1939, as well as a vivid recollection of being on Richmond station on 3 September of that year when air-raid sirens began to wail (a false alarm, as it turned out) and feeling that something very unpleasant was happening. Whatever the horrors of the war, the fact was that London Transport had by September 1939 become such a finely tuned, highly organised concern that it was able to cope in an admirable manner with the totally unprecedented demands placed upon it.

*Michael H. C. Baker*
Wareham
March 2007

# · 1 ·

# Four Great Men

JUST as there had been a considerable body of opinion in the first decades of the century which argued that the main-line railway companies should come under public control, so there were those who felt the same about public transport in the capital. The trauma of World War 1, if it had not brought about rail nationalisation, had resulted in the 'halfway house' of amalgamation into the Big Four in 1923, and when Labour won the general election of 1929 few doubted that changes were coming to London too. Our story is dominated by four men, who, ably assisted by many others, ranging from those in positions of considerable power — managers, engineers, designers, administrators — right through to the drivers, conductors, motormen, ticket collectors, porters etc who were in everyday contact with the travelling public, were instrumental in creating what, it is generally agreed, was by 1939 the most forward-looking and best-organised transport undertaking of any capital city. The four were Herbert Morrison, Charles Holden, Lord Ashfield and Frank Pick.

Herbert Morrison was a Londoner through and through. Born in Lambeth in 1888, he left school at 14. His parents were working people, sufficiently well off to afford an annual week's holiday in Ramsgate. As he wrote in his autobiography, 'Secondary education was hardly thought of by parents of my class and time', and he took up work as an errand-boy in a shop. Always interested in politics, he sought ways of bettering both himself and working people generally. The loss of sight in his right eye meant he did not serve in World War 1, to which he was anyhow opposed, arguing that the working men of Britain and Germany had much in common. A founder member of the London Labour Party, by 1920 he had become Mayor of Hackney; two years later he was elected to the London County Council, and in 1923 he entered Parliament as MP for South Hackney. Defeated in the 1924 election, he returned to Parliament in the Labour victory of 1929 and was appointed Minister of Transport by Prime Minister Ramsay MacDonald.

Morrison, with his trade-union background, was somewhat wary of handing over the assets of the LCC to 'Lord Ashfield and his wicked Combine', as he once wrote, but he was also a realist, warning against favouring any one form of transport against another and stating that he would be 'guided by the facts'. In December 1929 he announced that it was the Government's view that public ownership of transport in London must be established, and, despite his earlier comments about Ashfield, it is generally agreed that the two were instrumental in the foundation of the London Passenger Transport Board (LPTB).

*Above:* The Prince of Wales (later Edward VIII) and Lord Ashfield on an Underground train during a Royal visit in 1935. *London's Transport Museum*

*Left:* A wartime David Low cartoon of Herbert Morrison, second from right in the front row, alongside Ernest Bevin, Clement Attlee and Winston Churchill. The title was 'All Behind You'.

Morrison refused to serve in MacDonald's National Government of 1931, which relied upon Conservative support, and instead devoted his formidable energies to the London County Council, becoming its leader in 1934, by which time London Transport was a *fait accompli*. He returned to Parliament in 1935, and by 1940 he was Deputy Leader of the Labour Party and Home Secretary under Winston Churchill in the wartime coalition, being still very much concerned with the fate of Londoners, especially during the Blitz, when the East End suffered grievously.

Serving between 1945 and 1951 as Deputy Prime Minister, Leader of the House of Commons and Foreign Secretary, Morrison could be hard and ruthless and had enemies in his own party as well as amongst his opponents. Eileen Wilkinson, the first woman to serve in a Labour government (and, according to Hugh Dalton, Chancellor of the Exchequer, 'a devoted worshipper of Herbert Morrison'), described

him as 'an able administrator' but 'a bit of a brute — the rudest man I know', conceding that 'he is giving to London almost exclusively gifts needed by the nation'. It was once remarked of Morrison that he was his own worst enemy. 'Not while I'm around', was the riposte of arch enemy Ernest Bevin, Foreign Secretary in the 1945-51 Labour Government but who as leader of the Transport & General Workers' Union in the 1920s and '30s had had many dealings with the London Transport management. With his John Lennon-type glasses and Tintin-like quiff, Morrison was a gift to cartoonists. One of the towering political figures of the first half of the 20th century (and the grandfather of Peter Mandelson), he remained active in politics, latterly as a life peer, until his death in 1965.

Lord Ashfield was Chairman of the LPTB from 1933 until 1947, and Frank Pick was his Chief Executive from 1933 until 1940. To quote Sir John Elliot, Chairman from 1953 to 1959, 'It was the combination of Pick and Ashfield, rather than the work of either, that brought about the remarkable development of public transport in the 30 years prior to the outbreak of war in 1939. The two men were essentially complimentary; Ashfield was best in dealing with politicians, shareholders and the public. Pick, on the other hand, was a very shy man, but he had great qualities as an administrator.'

Albert Stanley, 1st Baron Ashfield, came from a humble enough background, his father being a Derbyshire coachbuilder who had emigrated to

9

was appointed its publicity officer. Although a solicitor by profession, he soon revealed a remarkable sense of design, such that, in a tribute after his death in 1941, he was described by Nikolaus Pevsner as 'the greatest patron of the arts whom this century has so far produced in England and indeed the ideal patron of our age'. Like Charles Holden, Frank Pick spurned honours, refusing both a knighthood and a peerage. He worked extremely long hours, often ending his day in the early hours with a 'spot inspection' of a station to check that the most detailed aspects — signs, litter bins etc — had been completed correctly.

Pick encouraged artists, many of them amongst the most progressive, to produce posters and good design in every aspect of public transport. He was founder member of the Design & Industries Association and founding chairman of the Council for Art & Industry, the forerunner of the Arts Council. His achievements gained international recognition, perhaps most extraordinarily in the form of an honorary Badge of Merit from the Soviet Union for his work on the Moscow Metro in 1932.

Chicago. Young Albert showed exceptional managerial skills, becoming head of the Detroit Street Railways by the age of 28, and in 1907, at the age of 33, was appointed General Manager of the Underground Electric Railways Co of London. Rapidly turning around its precarious financial position, he was appointed Managing Director in 1910. Knighted in 1914, he was appointed President of the Board of Trade during World War 1. In 1919 he returned to head the Underground Group, was created Baron Ashfield in 1920 and with Pick as Commercial Manager established a unique partnership, the benefits of which are still felt by anyone who travels by bus, tram or train in London today. It was indeed, as it has often been described, a 'Golden Age'. In 1928 Lord Ashfield handed over the role of Managing Director to Pick, remaining Chairman and concentrating on the complex, long-drawn-out negotiations that led to the setting-up of the LPTB.

Frank Pick, four years younger than Stanley and born into a devout Congregationalist family in Lincolnshire, had joined the Underground Group in 1906 — a year earlier than Stanley —and in 1908

In many respects Ashfield and Pick *were* London Transport in the 1930s, and, reading of their achievements, from such seemingly minor examples as the introduction in 1935 of compulsory bus stops to their worldwide fame, and their characters, so different yet so perfectly complementary, one is simply lost in admiration. Frank Pick resigned in 1940 and was appointed by Winston Churchill as Director of Information. Sadly he died the following year, aged 62, no doubt worn out by his Herculean efforts. Lord Ashfield died in 1948, aged 74.

Charles Holden, the architect responsible for the London Transport building style of the 1930s, was a most interesting man. He had a strong social conscience, twice refusing a knighthood because he believed 'architecture should be a collaborative effort'. Born in Bolton in 1875, he did not have things easy as a child, his father going bankrupt and his mother dying when he was six. Studying in Manchester, he

was trained in the classical tradition, of which he was a master, and from this he developed a style based on a deep respect of materials and the function of a building. Thus he saw no need of 'cornices, pilasters, mouldings . . . when in doubt leave it out'.

Very much influenced by the post-1914 generation of Northern European masters — Arnos Grove station, for instance, is based on Gunnar Asplund's Stockholm City Library — Holden had a huge influence in Britain and, to a degree, abroad. A man of ascetic habits, he was practically hero-worshipped by his colleagues. 'Fitness for purpose' was his creed. Buildings should take account of their surroundings, be aware of their function. Their interiors and their fittings (lamps, escalators, ticket offices and shop façades) were as important as their exteriors — something which has been adhered to pretty faithfully in the decades since the Morden extension, the rebuilt Piccadilly station and all the rest that were erected. Few architects of the 20th century have had a greater impact on London than Holden, for he also designed what is now Zimbabwe House in the Strand (almost opposite Charing Cross station), 55 Broadway, completed in 1929 and which in 1933 would become the headquarters of London Transport, and, most spectacular of all, Senate House, the administrative headquarters of the University of London and described at the time as 'London's first skyscraper'.

# · 2 ·

# The Workers

Possibly just about the toughest job on London Transport, a points operator at a tramway junction. In later years this tended to be the responsibility of uniformed inspectors who were given a canvas shelter to keep out of the worst of the weather.
*London's Transport Museum*

MORRISON and the LCC as a whole were much concerned with unemployment, which was a persistent problem throughout the 1920s and '30s. Received wisdom is that it grew much greater after the Wall Street Crash of 1929, but it had existed ever since soldiers returning from World War 1 found that 'a land fit for heroes' could not necessarily provide them with a job. London and the South East was not as hard hit as the industrial North, the Midlands or South Wales; in 1932 some 5% of males were unemployed in London, whilst in parts of the North the figure could be as high as 33%. But the fear of unemployment was ever present, and there was relatively little industrial agitation; which is not to say that it was entirely absent. In *A Lifetime of Bus Work* (Transport Publishing Co, 1979), Bob Scanlan, who worked in the machine shop at Chiswick in 1932, recalls hearing 'through the grapevine' that redundancies were on the way; one of his colleagues, 'a skilled man and an ex-apprentice of the company', found himself sweeping station platforms for £2 a week.

With the full effects of the downturn in business hitting London's bus, tram and Underground services it was announced that there would be a cut in wages. The Transport & General Workers' Union, led by Ernest Bevin, reluctantly accepted this, but a number of his members did not, and early in 1933 a militant group called a strike in which between 20 and 30 bus garages took part. Negotiations continued and the strike was called off. The Communist party newspaper, *The Daily Worker,* backed the strike action and accused Bevin and the Union leaders of being 'agents of the management' and 'fighting for the company against the men, Bevin sued for libel — and won.

A number of the leaders of the militants were Communists — or sympathetic to Communist ideals — at a time when fascism was taking root in Germany, Italy and Spain, with adherents all over Europe. In Britain the charismatic Sir Oswald Mosley was active in the East End, provoking many who

A Central bus inspector stands sternly at the head of a queue whilst a business lady (possibly a stenographer) hurries by, newspaper under her arm. The inspector still wears an LGOC jacket, although the date is August 1934. *London's Transport Museum*

opposed his extreme-right-wing views to see Communism as the one force unequivocally prepared to stand up for the rights of workers everywhere, and throughout the 1930s there was a strong element within London's busmen which believed this and was prepared to act on it. The tram, trolleybus and railway workers seem to have been less militant.

An example of the differences manifested itself in May 1937, at the time of the Coronation of King George VI and Queen Elizabeth. Negotiations over a reduction in the working day had been dragging on for months. In late April the LPTB issued a definite 'No' but asked the Union to resume negotiations after the Coronation. The grievances were shared with busmen in many parts of the country, and there were strikes by employees at Maidstone & District, Eastern National and Luton Corporation, among others. The London tram men were sympathetic but not to the extent of striking. Bevin managed to persuade the provincial busmen to return to work whilst he negotiated their case, but the militant Londoners struck, no buses ran during the Coronation, and the Government set up a Court of Inquiry. Bevin spoke on behalf of the men, asserting that London Transport railwaymen had, in effect, the 7½-hour working day that the busmen wanted.

One of the strongest planks of Bevin's argument was that the harsh conditions of driving and conducting buses in London's streets was detrimental to the men's health and called doctors as witnesses of their nervous disorders. Frank Pick, in response, doubted the relevance of these assertions and said that the Board simply could not afford the £½ million that the reduction in working hours would cost. The findings of the Court were that the whole matter of conditions of work and the health of the employees should be properly investigated. The Executive Council of the Union declared this to be a '75-80% victory'. The strike ended on 28 May, and at a subsequent conference a number of the militants were expelled. One of them commented: 'I have never seen fascism operated so clearly!' Ironically, to quote H. A. Clegg in his book *Labour Relations in London Transport*, 'It was said that, owing to the crowds of Coronation Week, the buses were best off

*Right:* A Country Area inspector parks his BSA motor-cycle and checks an ST double-decker working the 417 somewhere in the Windsor area in January 1938. The motor-cyclist hardly seems to be appropriately attired for riding in the depths of winter. *London's Transport Museum*

*Below:* Driver and conductor of a Merton STL take refreshment from a Catering Department pedal-tricycle, Epsom, 1936. *London's Transport Museum*

the streets'. But the men had always claimed that it was mere coincidence that the strike occurred at this time, asserting that the Board could have settled the dispute much earlier.

Working in public transport was perceived as a job with considerable status; it was usually secure, and the uniform suggested the wearer exercised a certain authority. But it was no sinecure. In *Bare Empty Sheds* (Tramway & Light Railway Society, 1986) G. Harry Guilmartin recalls working with tram drivers from the inter-war years whose memories were of 'working long hours . . . in all weathers, often drenched, often frozen'. They had sometimes to suffer 'petty tyrants' who made their lives a misery, and a public complaint, 'probably unjustified or possibly untrue', might result in suspension and loss of wages.

The Unions were generally in favour of the creation of London Transport. Their leaders agreed with the directors of the Combine that 'wasteful competition' should be ended, that a unified authority meant greater prosperity for all, and that union representation was much weaker in the smaller concerns. There were worries about how members of the LPTB should be appointed, but these were generally allayed when John Cliff, Assistant General Secretary of the T&GWU was invited to join, even though he had to give up his union office to do so. The militant members, who called themselves the 'Rank and File Movement', were less impressed.

By and large most employees were not only content to work for London Transport but were even proud of doing so. Compared to many other employers London Transport treated its staff well. It provided various forms of welfare, and there were numerous sports clubs, drama groups and all manner of recreational activities in which wives and children were encouraged to take part. If 'Bonnie Baby' contests would nowadays be considered politically very incorrect, they are just one example of dozens if not hundreds of activities, some frivolous, some serious, that attracted contestants and spectators and were aimed at involving as many as possible, so that they would feel part of the London Transport family, however large this might be.

Six members plus the chairman made up the London Passenger Transport Board, appointed by, amongst others, the chairman of the London County Council, the chairman of the Committee of London Clearing Banks, the president of the Law Society and the president of the Institute of Chartered Accountants in England and Wales. It was clearly not an organisation to be taken lightly.

The welfare of staff (or, as the establishing Act describes them, 'officers and company servants') was a priority. No one 'shall, without his consent, be by reason of such transfer [to London Transport] in any

A guard gives the 'right away' to a Metropolitan Line train.
*Author's collection*

worse position in respect of the conditions of his service formerly obtaining'. Pensions were protected. The possible closure of the tramway system would have worried many LCC and borough employees. There was reassurance here. 'If . . . their services . . . are dispensed with by the Board upon the abandonment . . . of a tramway... that officer or servant shall, unless the contrary is proved, be deemed . . . to have suffered a direct pecuniary loss' and would be compensated.

Wages and salaries were not high, although they were sufficient to retain staff, particularly those doing shift work, who might have been tempted to look elsewhere. Anthony Bull, who rose to become Vice-Chairman of London Transport and received the CBE, recalled that he started with the Underground Group in 1929 as a Grade 5 Clerk on a salary of £120, rising to £130 a year later. A 16-year-old joining

*Above:* The typing pool, 55 Broadway, mid-1930s. *London's Transport Museum*

*Below:* The tracing section, Chief Engineer's drawing office, 55 Broadway, 23 August 1938. *London's Transport Museum*

*Above:* The proud LPTB mothers seem rather jollier, despite the inclement weather, than their bonny babies, c1936. Presumably these are the winners for the two on the left are clearly wearing rosettes. Note big brother attempting to get into the picture whilst being skilfully elbowed into the background. *London's Transport Museum*

*Left:* An interesting variation, perhaps unique to London Transport, on the egg-and-spoon race, photographed around the same time. *London's Transport Museum*

*Left:* An elegant forehand shot performed, one suspects, especially for the camera, during a tennis tournament final at Keston sports ground with a pair of LT six-wheelers parked on the adjoining road, 10 September 1933. *London's Transport Museum*

the Underground as a clerk in 1939 would have started at £55 per annum, this rising to £90 at the age of 18. At the other end of the scale a Class 1 clerk could reach £345 per annum after two years in that grade. For some reason women's salaries were quoted in weekly terms rather than yearly. A 16-year-old received 21s 6d (£1.07½) per week, virtually the same as her male counterpart. A Class 1 lady clerk, after two years in this grade, received 71s 6d (£3.57½) per week, which works out at £371 per annum — considerably more than her male counterpart, which is most surprising. An Underground ticket collector (Class 1) was paid 62s 6d (£3.12½) per week, a porter a maximum 56s 6d (£2.82½) per week.

A Central Area bus driver's wage after 18 months' service was 90s (£4.50) per week, a conductor's 84s 0d (£4.20). Their average working time was 6hr 27min a day. A tram or trolleybus crew worked rather longer, 7hr 10min a day, drivers and conductors both being paid 84s per week. The maximum wage for a Country Area bus driver was 75s (£3.75), for his conductor 66s 6d (£3.32½); they worked 6hr 59min a day.

Many LPTB employees took more than a passing interest in their vehicles and trains, and, although in the 1930s there was nothing like the enthusiast movement of today, there were certainly those who studied, noted, photographed and wrote about the bus, tram, trolleybus and train fleets, despite information being much harder to come by than it would be once the Ian Allan 'ABCs' began to appear in the next decade.

*Above:* Two Central Area bus conductors pose in winter uniform, 1935. *London's Transport Museum*

Most, whether observers or employees, understood the realities and did not wear rose-tinted spectacles. They appreciated that what might bring joy to the enthusiast would be seen in a different light by the ordinary passenger. G. Harry Guilmartin describes being regularly sick as a child on the Underground: 'I think it was the unpleasant smell the trains had in those days.' He was similarly afflicted on buses, by 'petrol fumes, dusty upholstery and Lord knows what else'. One sometimes hears elderly folk complaining that public transport is not as comfortable as it was. It is easy to forget what an unhygienic, pungent world it was in the 1930s when homes with hot running water were the exception, when few people bathed more than once a week, when we were generally poorer, changed our clothes far less often, and when cigarette fumes impregnated upholstery and clothing.

*Right:* A conductor with a white-topped (summer uniform) hat helps a lady passenger aboard his Central Area LT c1935. *Author's collection*

*Below left:* Looks a lot worse than it is. A volunteer demonstrates how to be run over by STL1143 whilst watched by a truly horrified (honest!) group of onlookers, none of whom have been dragged away from their otherwise gainful employment in various parts of Chiswick Works c1937.
*London's Transport Museum*

*Below:* Whatever the first glance at this apparently rural idyll might indicate it is actually a scene at a suburban Underground station during an inspection (by Neville Chamberlain?) for best garden competition c1938.
*London's Transport Museum*

# • 3 •

# The Double-deck Bus Fleet
# in 1933 — before the Regent

THE most numerous double-deck bus type in the fleet on 1 July 1933 was the NS. In all 2,385 NSs had been built between 1922 and 1928, the LGOC's standard double-decker of the period. Although the majority came from the London General Omnibus Co (LGOC) a limited number was acquired from three other sources — London General Country Services, Thomas Tilling and the British Automobile Traction Co (BAT).

At the beginning of 1930 1,781 of the NSs still had solid tyres and 61 were open-toppers. Withdrawal began in 1932, and by July 1933 183 had been taken out of service. Such was the pace of progress in bus design at the end of the 1920s and the early '30s that they already looked archaic, despite the majority having been modernised with pneumatic tyres and covered tops. Those which were missing one or other of these features looked even more out of date. Of 56

*Above:* Two NSs in George Street, Croydon, c1931. The one on the left, working on route 12 and bound for Oxford Circus, with conductor perched atop the staircase, is still without a roof whilst the one on the right, on local route 178, has this feature. *Author's collection*

*Left:* The first six-wheel double-deck motor bus to enter service in London was this 45-80hp Guy of the Public company, dating from 1927. It seated 60 passengers, and was finished in a predominantly blue livery. *Ian Allan Library*

working in the Country Area no fewer than 35 were without upper-deck roofs. The Tilling and BAT NSs did have tops but retained their solid tyres.

The chief feature of the NS which distinguished it from its predecessor, the S of 1920, was that it possessed a cranked (and therefore lower) chassis. This meant that passengers could step much more easily onto the rear platform and from there make just one more step into the lower saloon. It was also low enough to enable a roof to be fitted although that bastion of conservatism, the Metropolitan Police, refused to countenance this until March 1926. Although the NS was lower than the S there was still a significant gap between the bottom of the panelling and the road surface.

A total of 776 S types were at work on 1 January 1930 with London General, but all the red LGOC versions had been withdrawn before London Transport was created. There were six S types proper still in service with London General Country Services which lasted for just over a year with London Transport. Eleven examples of the PS, an East Surrey version of the S, were still in stock in July 1933, being needed for the 410, which ran from Bromley to Redhill beneath the famous (or perhaps infamous) low bridge at Oxted, although their successors were on order. Apart from their higher

floor level they did not look any more old-fashioned than the NS in its original form.

Predecessor to the S was the K, which came out immediately after World War 1, in 1919. These were London's first forward-control buses with the driver seated alongside the engine rather than behind it. In all 798 Ks were still at work in London on 1 January 1930, and rather remarkably 15 entered London Transport ownership, although all were delicensed and would be scrapped by the spring of 1934. These 15 had been retained to work on route 90 which passed over a bridge with severe weight restrictions, until June 1932.

The NS type, like its predecessors, was originally without windscreens — another police restriction —

One of the extraordinary-looking mammoth LS six-wheelers of the LGOC poses for the camera at Chiswick when brand-new. By 1930 all 11 LSs were working the 29, moving on to Cricklewood garage and the 16. Several were converted to lorries and survived World War 2. *Ian Allan Library*

and did not begin to acquire them until the late spring of 1931. Some were still without in 1933. When fitted with covered tops the upper deck window frames did not match up with those downstairs. Other features which dated them were their top-lights, a radiator which was as wide as it was high (and it certainly was high), whilst the front wings were pretty minimal. Only the Country Area NSs had headlamps, and although the downstairs seat cushions were quite deep there was little else in the way of comfort, with plenty of protrusions likely to catch the unwary passenger as he or she either made for his or her seat or rose to leave it.

Similar to the NS but several steps ahead of it was the LS, introduced in 1927. The LSs were actually ADCs rather than AECs, although all had (either from new or shortly afterwards) AEC engines. The

LGOC's first six-wheelers, they were built new with an enclosed upper deck, an enclosed staircase and pneumatic tyres. There were seats for 60 passengers, later reduced to 56. The 11 LS double-deckers and one single-decker are said to have been less than entirely successful, but for all that they worked the 16 group of routes from Cricklewood garage for 10 years, finally being withdrawn at the same time as the very last NSs. Four were then converted as break-down tenders and in this form lasted well into the postwar era, not being withdrawn until April 1951.

ADC was the result of a brief amalgamation of AEC and Daimler. AEC had always supplied the vast majority of London's buses and would do so right up until the late 1960s, but although Daimlers would make a comeback during World War 2 (and again in the late 1960s) a mere five double-deck Daimlers entered the LPTB fleet in 1933, and all were gone two years later — well, sort of. Three rather sophisticated CH6s with epicyclic gearboxes and fluid-flywheel transmission were bought as an experiment by the LGOC in 1931 and fitted with standard ST bodies. They influenced the later versions of the AEC ST and LT types, but they

*Above:* WR20, a Sunbeam 70/142hp six-wheeler of the Westminster company working route 73, August 1933. Impressive and up-to-date the bus may be in most respects, but it is rather let down by the Metropolitan Police's insistence that the driver be exposed to the elements. *Ian Allan Library*

*Left:* An NS in original condition with solid tyres affords the upper-deck passengers an unrestricted view of the glorious Surrey countryside on its way to Hook in the summer of 1930. *Pamlin Prints*

*Left:* Covered-top, pneumatic-tyred NS1445 of Chalk Farm garage stands beside the Crystal Palace c1933. *Author's collection*

*Below:* An archaic-looking Thomas Tilling normal-control petrol-electric near New Cross ahead of a General NS, with solid tyres but upper-deck roof, both on their way to Chislehurst c1930. *W. Noel Jackson*

*Left:* A bowler-hatted gentleman, carrying an intriguingly shaped parcel, boards a covered-top NS on route 24 near Trafalgar Square c1932. *Ian Allan Library*

*Below:* Contrast in design. By the mid-1930s the outside-staircase NS looked archaic and far removed from this light, airy, functional bus shelter in Epsom. *London's Transport Museum*

themselves soon departed, the chassis being sold and the bodies being transferred to new AEC chassis. These were placed in the STL class, which was highly confusing to bus spotters, as they looked like STs and were the same length as STs. Two further Daimlers were acquired from independents, and were soon sold.

World War 2 Daimlers were placed, logically, in the D class, but this could not be done in 1933 as this letter was reserved for the more numerous Dennis double-deckers. These were four-ton normal-control buses owned by various independents, 69 of which were at work in 1930. Not surprisingly the LPTB got shot of the 26 it acquired, all being withdrawn by the end of July 1935. There were also some rather more

*Left:* The very last run by an NS in passenger service (there were just four left, working peak-hour route 166 from West Green garage), captured by the LT official photographer on the evening of 30 November 1937. *London's Transport Museum*

*Below:* A scene full of interest, recorded at Mile End in 1931. Of the many pedestrians, only one seems to be without headgear. Partly obscured by the tram-stop lamp-post is a six-wheel bus of intriguing origin, for it is not an LT. *London's Transport Museum*

modern H-type forward-control Dennises, which London Transport classified DH. The LGOC had itself bought three in 1929 but found them inferior to the AEC LTs and STs. The rest of the type, 18 in total, came from independents, and all were gone by the end of May 1936.

Finally, in the Dennis stable, was the Lance. This model was introduced in 1931 and did well enough nationwide against the otherwise all-conquering AEC Regent and Leyland Titan to remain in production into the 1950s. The LGOC bought 25 of the earliest examples, fitted them with ST-type bodies, classified them D and sent them to its subsidiary, Overground, at Potters Bar. Eight more came from independents; they too worked from Potters Bar, the whole class being now DLs. Transferred to Sutton at the end of 1936, these modern and efficient vehicles might have lasted until 1939 had not the busmen's strike of 1937 led to service cuts and their withdrawal at the end of November that year.

*Below:* Interesting use for a redundant double-deck bus. NS2052 was converted to a mobile betting shop at the Brooklands motor-racing track. *London's Transport Museum*

# • 4 •

# The All-conquering Regent

THE AEC Regent would be the standard London double-decker for the best part of 50 years. So we'll start with the Renown, which was simply a Regent with two extra wheels. (Even this needs qualifying, for in one sense a Regent also had six wheels, the back pair being actually doubles mounted one inside the other, but the Renown had one behind the other at the back; everyone could see it was a six-wheeler, and this is the accepted definition.) Had regulations not intervened there would have been no need for the Renown, for it was only restrictions on the length of a four-wheel chassis that brought about the 1ft-longer Renown.

LT1 seated 54 passengers, the next 149 of the type would seat 60 passengers, and most of the rest 56,

Open-staircase LT42 in original condition without a windscreen follows a Metropolitan NS in Trafalgar Square in 1930. *Author's collection*

except for the final, 'Bluebird' version, which, with the upper deck extended over the driver's cab, accommodated 60. In 1931 the police allowed the length of four-wheel chassis to be extended to 26ft, rendering the Renown redundant, and no more LTs entered service after 1932. Although basically a huge step forward from the NS in terms of its far superior interior, almost luxurious upholstery and permanent roof, the LT body had features that looked backwards, the most obvious being the outside staircase of the early examples and a frontal design with the upper deck set well back from the lower. The lucky drivers of LT1 were protected by a windscreen, but this caused a sharp intake of breath from the Metropolitan Police, which would not allow this civilised feature to become standard until March 1931. The majority of London's tram drivers had to put up with exposure to the elements for getting on for another 10 years.

The LT was modernised progressively throughout its three-year production run, enclosed staircases becoming standard from LT151 onwards, and a much more comprehensive route-number and destination display arriving in the latter half of 1931. LT345 had an inward curve to the upper-deck sides which became standard, whilst most dramatic was the appearance of LT741. This had the upper deck extended right over the cab (slightly ahead of it actually), and in essence the standard layout of the London half-cab double-decker had been arrived at. Mechanically, equally startling experiments and developments were afoot — Lockheed hydraulic brakes, the Wilson preselective gearbox and fluid transmission and the oil (diesel) engine being the most notable. Some 1,227 double-deck LTs were built, all of which passed into London Transport ownership. There was also a single-deck version, which we will consider elsewhere.

The prototype Regent entered service with East Surrey in July 1929 before moving on to Autocar; the first LGOC example, classified ST, was licensed in October of that year. What was so special about the Regent that London would fall in love with it and sustain the love affair for half a century? Simply that it was the best. It was designed by George Rackham, who had already produced the Titan and Tiger designs for Leyland, and between them the Regent and the Titan established a virtual monopoly of the British (and much of the overseas) double-deck market. The ST was in production between 1929 and 1932, the type totalling 1,137, being superseded by

*Above:* Two LTs, that on the left being of the final, 'Bluebird' variety, pass in Bow. In the distance can be seen are at least two more LTs, while just entering the picture (right) is an 'E1' tram. *London's Transport Museum*

*Below:* ST91 heads along the South East London tram tracks towards London Bridge on the 218 c1932. *Author's collection*

*Above:* An LT, ST437, a traffic policeman, and a choice selection of vehicles, including one horse-drawn (just about visible in front of the LT), in the Strand, 1932. *Arthur Ingram collection*

*Below:* A wonderful assortment of cloche hats, bowlers and bobbed hairstyles, plus an ST, c1931. *London's Transport Museum*

the longer but otherwise initially identical STL. The vast majority of the ST fleet looked exactly like a shorter version of the earliest standard type of enclosed-staircase LT, although there were, inevitably, a great many variations. Some, absorbed by London Transport from East Surrey and National, had square cabs, some round, with slightly smaller destination indicators. (Twenty years later a curious decision saw one of these smaller-indicator, round-cab versions selected to be the official preserved example, and when it went on display, painted red, at Clapham a number of faces turned the same colour, some with embarrassment, some with apoplexy.)

Unlike the Renowns, short-wheelbase Regents were acquired by London Transport from sources other than the LGOC. Some 191 came from Thomas Tilling. They looked completely different and distinctly old-fashioned, not least because they had open staircases. (Having said that, in December 2005 I travelled up from Cobham and toured the final Routemaster route, the 159, in the preserved example, ST922, and found its ride perfectly acceptable, even if

*Right:* The smiling Romford-based crew of ST154 (note the raised letters and numbers) pose in their summer uniform *c*1933. The *Sunday Pictorial* advert is a reminder that Hitler is about to assume power in Germany and that Lloyd George, Prime Minister during the latter days of World War 1, was, like Churchill, one of the few prominent politicians of the 1930s who early on saw the terrible dangers this presaged. *Alan B. Cross*

*Above left:* The lower deck of an ST. The protrusion of the long, straight staircase is particularly noticeable; also the gearbox casing upon which small boys with long legs sitting in the front seats used to love to place their feet in order to feel the vibrations; and *(right)* the beautifully designed, almost luxurious upper deck of an ST, with its generously padded seats. *London Transport*

*Top:* An AEC Regent of Chariot. An official LT picture taken shortly after passing into LPTB ownership in 1933. *Ian Allan Library*

*Above:* A Regent of the Lewis company ostensibly *en route* to Rickmansworth, 3 July 1930. *Pamlin Prints*

rather more fresh air was circulating than one normally expects in a 21st century bus.) There were also a handful of other open-staircase STs from independents, eight lowbridge examples which spent all their long lives (they would be the last STs to remain in service with London Transport) in the Amersham and Watford areas and, most handsome of all, 23 that were effectively ST (*i.e.* two-axle) versions of the LT 'Bluebird' and entered service with London General Country Services in 1932.

The successor to the ST was the 26ft-long STL. This was to be London's standard double-decker throughout the 1930s, although it would change greatly in appearance, evolving from something of an ugly duckling to one of the all-time classics. The first examples, following on directly from the last LTs, arrived in late 1932. Like the final LT design, the 'Bluebird' (so called because of the colour of its upholstery), the STL seated 60 passengers. It lacked the well-proportioned panache of the 'Bluebird' but served London well, the considerable increase in capacity over the 48-seat ST being much appreciated by operators if not passengers, for it was not as spacious, and the seats were less comfortable than those of the ST or the majority of LTs. An initial batch of 50 for the LGOC was followed by a further 100 buses, most of which entered service after the creation of London Transport. The other principal

constituent of the STL class upon the formation of London Transport was a batch of 80 built for Thomas Tilling. These bore some resemblance to the Tilling STs but were more modern, with completely enclosed, rather rounded bodies. However, to get the show on the road the driver still had to give the starting handle a hefty swing, making sure he didn't break his wrist in the process, and the engine was less powerful than that in the LGOC version; both shortcomings were soon addressed by London Transport. There were also six STLs inherited from independents.

The original LGOC STL1 design was succeeded in August 1933 by the very much better-looking and more comfortable 56-seat 3STL2. This had a sloping front and rounded back, a petrol engine and Daimler preselective gearbox and, although designed by the LGOC, was the first variation of the theme to be introduced by the newly formed London Passenger Transport Board. The seating capacity would remain standard for double-deckers right through the production run both of the STL and its successor, the RT.

Tilling STL93, lettered 'General', heads north at Victoria in 1934, passing 'E1' tram No 1528 which is about to return southeastwards, having got as far into the West End as trams were allowed. *Photomatic*

STL609, which entered service in November 1934, was the first example of the perfectly proportioned standard London double-decker of the later 1930s. To quote Ken Blacker, in his book entitled simply *The STLs* (Capital Transport, 1984), 'the gently curved frontal profile . . . was quickly copied by

Hendon garage in 1935. On the far left is an NS, which, despite the STLs now allocated to the garage, was still employed on one of Central London's most famous routes, the 13. In the centre of the picture is one of the 253-608 series of STLs dating from 1933/4, whilst on the right is one of the earliest examples built by the LGOC in 1932/3. *London's Transport Museum*

almost every other coachbuilder in the country'. The standard was set for the rest of the decade, although there would be many variations in chassis, engine and body. Diesel engines (or oil engines, as they were then known) were now standard. Whilst preparing this chapter I had the great good fortune to be introduced to Jack Lemmer, a remarkable centenarian who started work with the General in 1924 and was much involved with the STL. One of his projects was STL760, which was fitted with an automatic gearbox and sent to Merton garage. 'At the end of its first week in service I went down to see how it was performing,' recalled Jack. ' "I've got a complaint," said one of the drivers. "I don't know what to do with my left leg!".'

One variation of the standard STL was a forward-entrance version for the Country Area that followed on from some forward-entrance lowbridge examples (with provincial Weymann bodies) which worked the 410 from Godstone garage. Another comprised a batch with heavily domed roofs and strengthened tyres for working through the Blackwall Tunnel. Then there was an oddity, in the shape — that being the operative word — of STL857, which, in keeping with the times, was given a streamlined full-front and was renumbered STF1. It was neither pretty nor practical.

Best remembered of all was the roofbox variety, which appeared in the spring of 1937. Meccano Dinky Toys, whose products were deeply desired by every boy with sufficient pocket money (or an indulgent uncle), brought out a model of this; although never identified as such and not painted in London colours, a roofbox STL was clearly what it was, thus ensuring that the design achieved near-immortality. Similar in appearance to the standard

Specially modified STL1866 with domed roof and reinforced tyres emerges from the north portal of the Blackwall Tunnel shortly after replacing NSs on this service in 1937. *Ian Allan Library*

STLs were the 100 Leyland Titan TD4s of the STD class, their Leyland bodywork being skilfully disguised to look very like the standard Chiswick product.

The entry into service of the very last standard STL, STL2647, coincided with the outbreak of World War 2. This did not, however, immediately bring double-deck bus production to an end, for already the STL's successor, the RT, had appeared. Much has been written about this superb vehicle, without doubt the finest half-cab, rear-entrance 56-seat double-decker ever built. Suffice to say here that, although RT1 entered service in August 1939, the vast majority of the 4,825 eventually built for London service appeared between 1947 and 1954.

*Above:* Streamlined, full-fronted STL857 before renumbering as STF1, January 1936. *London Transport*

*Right:* Q2. It bears some (although not a particularly striking) likeness to the full-fronted STL. *Ian Allan Library*

*Above:* A lady hails STL901 at one of the newly installed standard LT request stops in the Strand in the summer of 1937. *London's Transport Museum*

*Below:* Cricklewood garage in the winter of 1938 with a line of STLs and STs, all wrapped up and prepared for whatever the weather might inflict. Nearest the camera is roofbox STL2037, delivered in March 1937, next is STL856 of August 1935. *London's Transport Museum*

*Above:* Although more and more middle-class families now owned a car, causing huge traffic jams at weekends on the largely inadequate main roads leading into and out of London, the vast majority of the population still relied on public transport. Crowds queue patiently beside 1938-built STL2403 on the edge of Epping Forest, 29 May 1939. *London's Transport Museum*

*Right:* Changing styles as the end of the decade approaches. The bobbed haircuts and cloche hats of the early 1930s had quite vanished by the time this picture was taken of office workers heading across London Bridge in 1939. A Tilling ST, a standard STL and two STs go about their business. *London's Transport Museum*

*Right:* The Lawn Tennis Championships at Wimbledon have always generated vast crowds of train and bus travellers. Hats are more prominent in this June 1939 view. *London's Transport Museum*

*Above:* Another view of the crowds waiting for a bus home, which looks like being an STL, from the Royal Forest Hotel, Chingford, after spending Whit Monday (29 May) 1939 in Epping Forest. Interestingly very few are wearing hats. *London's Transport Museum*

*Left:* The shape of things to come. The white-coated driver of RT1 sits upright and vigilant in charge of the prototype of what many consider to be the finest bus design ever to run in London — a service provided for 40 years, from 1939 to 1979. *London's Transport Museum*

# The Single-deckers

To some extent the London single-deck fleet had its double-deck equivalents; but there were plenty of exceptions, not least because right through the 1930s experiments were being conducted, in close co-operation with AEC and Leyland, on where to place the engine, these being confined, with one exception, to single deck chassis. The single-deck version of AEC's Regent was the Regal. This remained in production right through the decade, and although there were many variations all were placed in the T class. The first entered service in 1929, and 370 came into LPTB stock. These were

T116 and forward-entrance STL980 inside Chelsham garage c1936. Green Line livery and lettering was subject to constant variation at this time.
*Author's collection*

Central and Country Area buses and a very large number of Green Line coaches.

The beginning of the Green Line adventure is very much the story of the early versions of the T class, for although a number of different makes operated under the Green Line umbrella in its early days it was the T class that was dominant. The first was T38, quickly followed by another 250 in 1931. Their bodies were built by a number of manufacturers, and whilst they were not all identical they were all built to a very similar, Chiswick-inspired style. Green Line was set up by the LGOC in 1930 as it became aware that it was losing traffic to a number of independents that had tapped into the demand for travel from the Country Area into Central London. The creation of London Transport simplified the situation, and by the beginning of 1936 a complex network of regular

*Left:* T217. This 1/7T7/1 variant with standard Chiswick-designed bodywork, dating from 1930, was an absolute classic. Although soon rendered obsolete by the magnificent 10T10s and lasting on Green Line work for less than 10 years, these coaches never lost their looks, and (as may be judged from the restored T219) in their livery of two-tone of green and black, with chromium embellishments, they looked superb.
*London's Transport Museum*

*Below:* Green Line T232. Although dating from 1931, in this picture it sports its unique all-metal 35-seat Metro-Cammell body, fitted in 1933 after an accident. *The Omnibus Society*

*Above:* T309, a Hall Lewis-bodied AEC Regal of 1930, delivered to East Surrey. *London's Transport Museum*

*Below:* London General S439 in Cheam High Street. Dating from 1921, the vehicle had the driver exposed to the elements. This outer-suburban 113 route bore absolutely no relation to the double-deck 113, which terminated at Oxford Circus. S439 managed to survive until July 1935, by which time it looked extraordinarily antiquated compared with the modern Chiswick-designed single-deckers then entering service. *Pamlin Prints*

10T10 T505 poses in the early spring of 1938 before entering service on route C1. There could be no more fitting destination than Tunbridge Wells for a vehicle of such classic proportions. *London's Transport Museum*

services, identified by letters, extended around the compass from Tilbury, Brentwood, Ongar and Bishop's Stortford in the east by way of Baldock, Hitchin, Luton, Dunstable, Aylesbury, High Wycombe, Windsor, Ascot, Guildford, Horsham, East Grinstead, Tunbridge Wells and back to the Thames Estuary at Gravesend. Various stopping places were established in the West End, notably, in the early days, Poland Street coach station, near Oxford Circus, but it was Eccleston Bridge, above Victoria railway station and a few yards from London Coastal Coaches' Victoria terminus, with which Green Line was most commonly associated.

Although two experimental Green Line double-deckers — an LT and a Q — were tried out, single-deckers were the norm, with successive variations on the T-type theme dominant.

Among its predecessors was the S class, which consisted of 64 solid-tyred 30-seat buses dating from 1922-4 plus a further 14, with pneumatic tyres, built for National in 1928. Of the 58 acquired by London Transport all had gone by January 1937 (although a remarkable sight on the HCVC London–Brighton run of 2005 which took practically everyone by complete surprise was that of newly restored S433, most enthusiasts not even being aware of its existence).

In the late 1920s AEC and Daimler products were marketed as ADCs. Exactly 100 coaches and buses of this make passed to the LPTB in 1933, most of which had gone by the end of 1936. Among the ADCs were the earliest examples of AEC's Reliance

model, introduced in 1927. Althogether 49 Reliances came into London Transport stock, the last being taken out of service by the end of January 1939.

Single-deck Renown buses received the same classification (LT) as their double-deck counterparts. Some 202 were acquired by London Transport, and all were still at work as 1940 opened. Although production of the LT class ended in 1932 and sales of the Renown went into deep decline nationwide with the easing of restrictions on the length of a four-wheel chassis, a little surprisingly another 34 Renown single-deckers were placed in service in 1937/8. Classified LTC, they were 30-seat private-hire coaches with Weymann bodywork and looked very like the 10T10 Green Line coaches. The six-wheel chassis, with less wheel-arch intrusion into the body, was chosen with comfort in mind; they were also given petrol engines to keep noise levels to a minimum.

The LPTB's most numerous single-decker was the 10T10, a slightly modified version of the 9T9 of 1936. Weymann-bodied Green Line coaches, the 50 9T9s were nice-looking vehicles apart from a rather clumsy-looking built-up front end; in the event they did very little Green Line work, being demoted to Country Area buses within three years. The 10T10 has always been regarded as a classic design. There were 266 of them, fitted with 30- or

*Right:* Q43. Placed in service in August 1935, this side-engined, 37-seat BRCW-bodied bus of revolutionary design was destined to serve in the Country Area for the best part of 20 years. *R. J. Snook*

*Below:* Rather less beautiful — but then revolutions seldom are. The prototype underfloor-engined Leyland Tiger TF1. It also carries Tunbridge Wells side route boards but these were probably fixed for photographic purposes as it is also sporting trade plates. *London Transport*

FJJ 617

34-seat composite bodywork (a tidied-up version of the 9T9), and they replaced all Green Line vehicles pre-dating the 9T9s.

The Q was an AEC innovation, a breakaway from the traditional engine-at the front layout, and London Transport owned far more than all other operators put together. The prototype, Q1, had an LGOC body, but the first production vehicles were 102 buses with slightly odd-looking 35 seat bodies, higher at the front than at the back, and went into service in 1935/6. Although intended for bus use in the Country Area, some worked for a short while as Green Line coaches. Next came 80 vehicles designed for Central Area service, although some initially worked in the Country Area. They were in one important respect the direct link with the postwar RFs, for they had the entrance ahead of the front wheels, beside the driver. Fifty Green Line coaches followed in 1936/7, bringing the grand total of single-deck Qs to 233.

The Q was followed by two more designs with unconventional engine positions, both of which appeared in 1937. The TF was a modified Leyland Tiger, with the engine mounted beneath the floor. The first had the oddest-looking cab imaginable; like something out of 1930s science fiction, it was practically all-glass and was seemingly designed by someone who had not the slightest interest in what the rest of the vehicle looked like. Next came 12 private-hire coaches; with deep windows, glass roof panels and well-proportioned cab these were truly beautiful vehicles, but sadly all but one were destined to be destroyed during the Blitz. Finally came 75 Green Line coaches. All TFs bar the prototype dated from 1939.

The other innovation of 1937 was the rear-engined Leyland Cub, 49 of which formed the CR class. All had bus bodywork very much in the Chiswick tradition of the late 1930s. Neither the TF nor the CR took advantage of their respective engine positions, both types retaining the conventional half-cab layout. There were two earlier Cub varieties. First came 96 front-engined, normal-control buses, one-man 20 seaters, for both Central and Country work; C1 appeared in 1934, the rest in 1935. Eight quite different buses went into service in 1936. These were forward-control one-and-a-half-deckers, painted in an attractive blue and cream livery and used on the 'Inter Station' service between the main-line termini.

*Above:* The career of the CR class of rear-engined Leyland Cubs would span 15 years. In the twilight of their lives several were transferred to the Country Area and repainted green; allocated to Epping, CR10 is seen in Hoddesdon in the late 1940s. *Ian Allan Library*

*Left and below left:* The neat interior of one of the CR class . *London Transport*

*Right:* Leyland Cub C26 poses at Chiswick on a wet day in May 1935 before being sent off up north to work the 303. According to the contemporary caption on the back of this photograph the C class was delivered at the rate of six a week from May 1935.
*Ian Allan Library*

*Above:* C106 posed at Chiswick in all its blue-and-cream glory on delivery in 1936.
*Ian Allan Library*

*Left:* Looking towards the rear of Inter Station forward-control Cub C106. The interior fittings show how closely related was the RT to the single-deck fleet of the later 1930s. *Ian Allan Library*

*Left:* Dennis Dart DA9, the standard LGOC small bus of 1930-3. The 226 ran between Cricklewood and Golders Green station. *Norman Hamshere*

newer vehicles, all being out of service by December 1939. London Transport also acquired 45 larger Dennis single-deckers, which it quickly disposed of. Also disposed of were the 42 Leyland Tigers and 21 Titans fitted with single-deck bus or coach bodywork which the LPTB had inherited from various sources.

Gilfords had been very popular in the 1920s and very early '30s, and London Transport acquired no fewer than 220. However, Gilford could not compete with the Tiger and the Regal and folded in 1935. The LPTB had little use for these non-standard vehicles, with a variety of bus and coach bodies, and had disposed of all of them by the end of January 1938. Most found new owners, and some returned to London Transport service for a short while during the vehicle shortage of the late 1940s.

Twenty-seven Bedfords, most of them 20-seaters, came into the LPTB fold, and, perhaps surprisingly, a few lasted right through to 1939. Amongst a bewildering array of other single-deck types, some long forgotten and all quickly removed from the LPTB fleet, were Albions, Bristols, Beans, Chevrolets, Commers, Daimlers, Fords, Dodges, Guys, Lancias, W&Gs, Thornycrofts, Tilling-Stevens, Karriers, Lafflys, Manchesters, AJSs, GMCs, Morrises, Reos, Saurers, Stars, one BAT, one Brockway, one International, one Minerva, one Overland, and one British Associated Transport Cruiser (!).

Predecessors of the Cubs were the LGOC Dennis Darts of 1930-3 (42 of them, with Chiswick-designed 20-seat bodies) plus three inherited by London Transport in 1934 from Romford & District. They were replaced towards the end of the decade by

*Below:* A delightful study of a Rayner's Horsham Bus Services normal-control Vulcan at Horsham Carfax in 1930. It is clearly in no hurry to depart, for there is no sign of a driver and the lady with the bicycle seems to be engaged in conversation with one of the passengers through the window which, on what is clearly a very warm summer's day, has been dropped right down. By the end of 1933 practically all the many routes serving Horsham were divided between the LPTB, Southdown and Aldershot & District, although the independents always kept a toehold. *Pamlin Prints*

*Above:* A little Dennis Ace with 20-seat Waveney body, BPF 318, ordered by Gravesend & District but delivered to London Transport in March 1934, climbs through the Chilterns. It was sold by the LPTB after a mere four years' service. *London's Transport Museum*

*Below:* Hertford garage in October 1935: as varied a selection of single-deckers as one could wish for, plus a 'Bluebird' ST and two NSs. *London Transport*

# • 6 •

# The Underground, Metropolitan and District Lines

The trains that the London Transport Passenger Board found itself operating on that July day in 1933 were a very mixed bunch. They ranged from metal, riveted 'Tube' stock, which looked as if it had been built from left-over bits of 'Dreadnought' battleships, through wooden-bodied surface carriages that had somehow got diverted from their intended destination of Coney Island and were now more familiar with Sloane Square, to several of the archaic original Beyer Peacock 4-4-0Ts, put out to grass in the rural fastness of the Brill branch, and smooth-looking 'Tube' and surface stock with automatic sliding doors — and, most incongruously, two Pullmans, called *Mayflower* and *Galatea*.

Without its complex network of electric railways, running at various depths beneath the streets of the City, the West End and the inner suburbs, London would, by 1933, have pretty well come to a halt. In 1932 this network carried 498 million passengers, a

figure more or less evenly divided between the 'Tube' and the surface lines. It might be as well to make sure that when we refer to surface stock we mean the trains which worked the Metropolitan, Inner Circle (as the Circle Line was then called) and District lines (which of course, spent much of their time below the surface but not as far down as the 'Tube' lines) and which in their dimensions were more or less comparable to main-line vehicles. 'Tube' trains were considerably smaller. Which, incidentally, meant that the electrical traction equipment had to be above floor level, thereby restricting the amount of space for passengers. One of the many innovations London Transport would introduce in the 1930s would be a solution to this problem.

The Metropolitan was the very first underground railway in the world, its original section, from Bishops Road, Paddington, to Farringdon, in the City, opening on 10 January 1863. By 1864 the first

*Left:* Difficult to believe that this rural idyll has any connection with the London Underground system, but this is the Metropolitan's 4.4pm from Quainton Road passing Wood Siding in high summer, 22 June 1935, hauled by one of the original 4-4-0Ts. *H. C. Casserley*

*Right:* A year earlier Mrs Casserley smiles for Henry's camera at Chesham with an 0-4-4T heading the branch train. *H. C. Casserley*

of the famous Beyer Peacock 4-4-0Ts was in service. Although long displaced from the capital by electrification, five managed to survive into the 1930s, mainly for the Brill branch. As John Glover records in *London's Underground* (Ian Allan Publishing, 1999), 'The train was sometimes quite empty, in which case the crew would often stop and go rabbiting in the woods'. Can one imagine a greater contrast than with the hustle and bustle 30-odd miles away around the Inner Circle? (One can get something of the flavour of this today if one stands on the platform at Quainton Road, where the Brill branch connected with the rest of the system and where preservationists have done a most sensitive job in re-creating a rural junction deep in the Buckinghamshire countryside.) Not surprisingly 55 Broadway soon put an end to this idyll: the branch closed on 2 December 1935, and the rabbits were left in peace — or perhaps the crews could now concentrate on harassing them. All but one of the 4-4-0Ts were scrapped, the lone survivor, No 23 (which in 1937 became L45) being found light duties in the service department until 1948. It had been somewhat modified over the years, the most noticeable alteration being the fitting of a cab. London Transport, pursuing its estimable preservation policy, then restored No 23, as it once again became, to a close approximation of its 19th-century days working underground.

The Metropolitan was the most distinctive of London Transport's railways, being in some respects more like a main line, with its goods yards, steam locomotives (some of them big, modern, Maunsell-designed 2-6-4Ts), electric locomotives and compartment-type carriages, as well as more conventional open-layout, sliding-door stock. It connected Central London with Uxbridge, Harrow and the Buckinghamshire towns of Rickmansworth, Amersham, Chesham and Aylesbury and on to Verney Junction.

For its territory beyond Swiss Cottage the Metropolitan Railway coined the term 'Metro-land', in doing so creating one of the most effective advertising ploys of all time. Colourful posters featuring neat, carefully set-out leafy estates of semi-detached 'Tudorbethan' villas complete with bow windows and add-on beams proved irresistible to city bank clerks, insurance salesmen, West End department-store managers and the like, and they moved in with their families throughout the 1920s and '30s, travelling to and from their places of work by, of course, the Metropolitan Line. It was a seemingly cosy, easily mocked world, but one must remember that many of the husbands would be survivors of the carnage of World War 1, and it was a way of life which the next generation would be prepared to fight and die for. It would later be celebrated with great affection by the Poet Laureate, Sir John Betjeman, who made a television programme (which still sells well as a DVD) of its delights, among them a man who had installed in his lounge — all 'Metro-land' houses had lounges — an electronic organ from a West End cinema, an ornithologist who proudly listed an astonishingly varied selection of birds found in a park in Neasden, and a Conservative ladies' luncheon (these ladies having been the young wives of 30 years earlier) featuring the finest collection of hats to be seen since the French Revolution.

As a child growing up in the 1940s I was fascinated by a picture in one of my big, colourful train books of a Metropolitan electric locomotive (I was familiar with electric multiple-units which were ten a penny in Thornton Heath, but an electric locomotive was something again) passing a bank of enormous poplar trees near bucolic-sounding Rickmansworth, although I was equally intrigued by Pinner (such an odd name), where Great Aunt May lived and whence she would visit us, travelling not by the Metropolitan Line but by trolleybus — which seemed to me an enormously long journey by this mode of transport. By the end of the 1930s London possessed the greatest trolleybus system in the world, and it was quite possible to make lengthy journeys all around suburbia. One of Betjeman's most evocative poems compares the hissing of the trolleys below Harrow-on-the-Hill with waves breaking on the shore in North Cornwall. The great illustrator W. Heath Robinson also lived for a time at Pinner and used to meet with his two

*Above:*
The photographer wrote on the back of this print: 'Old Metropolitan 0-6-2T No 93 makes quite a nice picture on a ballast train near Rickmansworth'. How right he was.
*F. R. Hebron*

*Left:* No 111, one of the handsome Maunsell-designed 2-6-4Ts, heads an up goods near Preston Road, Metropolitan Railway, in 1934.
*Ian Allan Library*

*Above:* A Metropolitan Railway 'H'-class 4-4-4T heads a five-coach train through the Chilterns north of Rickmansworth. *E. R. Wethersett*

*Right:* A Metropolitan Line Bo-Bo electric locomotive about to come off its train at Rickmansworth and hand over to steam for the rest of the journey to Aylesbury. *O. J. Morris*

illustrator brothers and friends in the Queen's Head, 'with its old oak panels and timbered ceilings' — a reminder that this was a village outside London until 'Metro-land' arrived. I never got to visit Pinner until Great Aunt May was long gone, together with daughter Wyn, who was married to Alf, known by the rest of the family as 'Know-all Alf' (although obviously not in front of Aunt May and Wyn). I, of course, was dying to meet him, for we were not a generally vindictive family, and for him to have

received such an epithet, I reasoned, his boasting must have been something to behold. Alas 'Know-all Alf' never accompanied Aunt May and Cousin Wyn on their epic trolleybus rides around the western suburbs, and I later began to wonder if perhaps there had been a parting of the ways. Divorce was not something our family, or indeed any family we knew, indulged in, and Mum never quite got over her beloved Prince of Wales' deserting the throne in 1936 to marry the divorced Wallis Simpson.

*Above:* A Hammersmith & City Line train of 'L' stock of 1931, photographed in July 1936. *Ian Allan Library*

*Right:* 'Day trip from Ravenscourt Park' is the title of this postcard depicting a school party of young ladies climbing aboard a District Line train. *London's Transport Museum*

*Far right:* A GWR '97xx' condensing pannier tank specially designed for working through the Underground tunnels heads past Paddington goods depot towards Smithfield with a train of 'Mica B' insulated meat vans c1938. *Author's collection*

The Hammersmith & City Railway dated back to 1864, when it had opened between Hammersmith and Green Lane Junction, Westbourne Park. For three years it was worked by the GWR, being taken over by the Metropolitan in 1867. In 1884 it was extended through Brunel's Thames Tunnel to New Cross, adjoining the SECR station, whilst the District shared most of the route, diverging south of the tunnel to the LBSCR New Cross station (which the Southern Railway would rename New Cross Gate). From 1905/6 the section between Shoreditch and the two New Cross stations was independently worked, by the East London Railway, still using steam-hauled trains. Electrification came in 1913, and through trains once again ran between Hammersmith and the two New Cross stations.

The District Line — the Metropolitan District, to give it its proper title — was similar in several ways to the Metropolitan, originating in 1868. It provided what would become the southern part of the Circle Line and gradually extended eastwards and westwards. It favoured the Beyer Peacock 4-4-0Ts which the Metropolitan Railway had introduced in 1864 and eventually owned 54 of them. Six survived electrification in 1905 and one, No 34, was still at work in 1930, its principal duty being to clear ice

from the conductor rails. It was withdrawn in 1932, replaced by a Hunslet 0-6-0T.

By the 1930s the District Line extended eastwards to Barking and then paralleled the LMS's London, Tilbury & Southend line as far as Upminster, which it reached in 1932. Built on the flat Essex marshes, this extension served a huge area covered mainly by council estates — an area, it must be said, rather lacking in character compared to 'Metro-land'. There, I've probably upset hundreds of nice Essex people now. Westwards it shared the Metropolitan route between Rayners Lane and Uxbridge — one of a number of branches from its main route out to Hounslow West. Other branches northwards were those to South Acton and Ealing Broadway. Southwards the Wimbledon line branched off at Earl's Court, whilst that to Richmond left the Hounslow line beyond Turnham Green. A feature of the District Line was that its several termini were situated alongside main-line stations. These were at Wimbledon, Richmond (which station would be rebuilt in the 1930s in distinctive art-deco style), Ealing Broadway, Kensington Olympia and Upminster. It was, of course, not unique in this respect, but the District seemed to have a particular affinity with above-surface routes.

# · 7 ·

# The 'Tube' Lines

THE City & South London (later Northern) Line incorporated London's first 'Tube' railway, which had opened in 1890 between the Elephant & Castle and the Bank. This was somewhat unusual; even now much the greater part of the 'Tube' system is north of the river. Powered, rather impractically, by locomotives, the carriages possessed tiny windows, not much bigger than the arrow slits in Norman castles, whilst the accommodation was scarcely more comfortable. The assumption was that, as there was nothing to see except unlit tunnels, who would want to look? This, like Bulleid with his notorious 'Tavern Cars' 50 years later, showed a profound ignorance of the basic desire of all train passengers to see where they are going, and especially which station they have arrived at; even in thick fog at midnight. Not that you get a lot of fog on the 'Tube', but you know what I mean. By 1930 the City & South London Line extended northwards to Highgate and Edgware and southwards to Morden. This made the Morden to Golders Green the longest tunnel in the world, as any right thinking schoolboy could have told you.

The Central London Railway, later the Central Line, opened in 1900, connecting the Bank, and soon, Liverpool Street, with Shepherd's Bush. This too was originally worked by locomotives, but these were soon ruled out of order, conversion to multiple-unit operation being effected in 1903. An extension was opened to Ealing Broadway in 1920, and others eastwards and westwards would be effected under London Transport control.

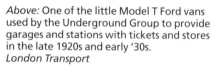

*Above:* One of the little Model T Ford vans used by the Underground Group to provide garages and stations with tickets and stores in the late 1920s and early '30s. *London Transport*

*Left:* Coming up. *London's Transport Museum*

*Above right:* Service vehicle V48 of the Underground's Commercial Advertising Department outside Lambeth North station. *London Transport*

*Right:* One wonders how the hats fared as these travellers, having posed for the flash camera, pushed their way into this clerestory roof, American-built 'Tube' train. *London Transport*

The Bakerloo Line began business on 10 March 1906, setting out from beneath the Metropolitan Railway station at Baker Street southwards by way of Waterloo to the Elephant & Castle and northwards to Edgware Road. In 1915 it expanded northwards to Queen's Park and two years later, using tracks built by the London & North Western Railway, to Watford. This was at that time far and away the furthest point north reached by 'Tube' trains.

The Piccadilly Line had also opened in 1906, running between Finsbury Park and Hammersmith. There had been no further extensions, but these were planned and would come about in the 1930s.

The Great Northern & City Railway ran from Finsbury Park to Moorgate. Opened on 14 February 1904, it was built to main-line dimensions, the intention being that Great Northern Railway trains should use it, but 70 years would elapse before this finally happened.

# • 8 •

# Curtains for the Trams — and What Might Have Been

THIS chapter is not about providing a more homely *ambience* for the tram fleet but about its impending doom. Throughout the 1920s there had been proposals to extend the LCC tram network. Elsewhere in Britain the future was far less rosy, and the motor bus was seen as a much more up-to-date, flexible, less costly alternative to the tram. The advent in 1927 of the first really successful double-deck chassis, the Leyland Titan, relatively low-floored by the standards of the time and with pneumatic tyres, hastened this process enormously. In 1931 the Royal Commission on Transport recommended that no more tramways should be built and that gradually motor buses and trolleybuses, running on wider, smoothly surfaced roads, many of them dual-carriageways and featuring roundabouts, would best provide public transport in the years to come. Meanwhile the LCC was building a fleet of new trams, which, whilst sturdy, well engineered and built to last, were nevertheless not much of an advance in the eyes of the general public on the traditional cars, the 'E1s', which dated back 30 years.

Yet there appeared in 1932 a completely different animal, a tram which not only looked different externally but which internally was light-years ahead of its immediate predecessors and rode like a dream.

This was No 1, and although I rode on it only once I saw it often and was immensely impressed. No 1 didn't just materialise on the streets of London one fine day in 1932: it must have been well into the planning stage when the 'HR2s' and the 'E3s' of 1930/1 were entering service, and I find it extraordinary that the LCC could not have held back for a year or so and then introduced a large fleet of 'No 1s', which together with the revolutionary 'Felthams' of the LUT and MET would have really given the anti-tram lobby something to think about.

In April 1929 *Tramway and Railway World* wrote: 'The greatest improvements yet effected in the double-deck tramway car have been credited to the three tramway companies operating in the Metropolitan area . . . The new car thus evolved may be said to constitute a model for the world.' Thus was the 'Feltham' introduced to a world grown cynical to the notion of steel rails in city streets. The magazine's claim was a huge one, but anyone who has sampled the delightful interior and riding qualities of prototype 'Feltham' No 331 at the National Tramway Museum at Crich — let alone those of my generation who every day rode the 'Felthams' through the streets of Croydon — will surely not disagree. The 'Feltham' had much in common with

the PCC car, introduced in the USA in the 1930s and taken up with enthusiasm in Europe. So successful was this design that it survived in its thousands long enough for the love affair with the tram or streetcar to revive worldwide from the 1980s onwards. Would the same have happened in London if, say, there had been 500 'Felthams' and 500 LCC 'No 1s' running by 1935? We cannot say, and in the event the beginning of the end for London trams came in 1931, when London United trolleybuses replaced trams operating in the Kingston, Twickenham and Hampton Court areas.

The first generation of London United trams was wearing out, as was the track. The Kingston area was not the most heavily used part of the network, so, whilst the company considered it worthwhile to invest in 'Feltham' trams for the profitable Uxbridge Road services, in 1929 experiments were conducted with trolleybuses; in 1931 authorisation was received to introduce them, and they took up work in May. Mounted on AEC chassis was bodywork built by the Union Construction Company at Feltham, a wholly owned Metropolitan Group subsidiary, and, despite having parts in common with the elegant 'Feltham' trams, the trolleybuses — 'Diddlers' as they came to be nicknamed, although no-one now seems to know

*Right:* The magnificent LCC No 1 in its original 'streamlined' blue livery. *Author's collection*

*Left:* Passengers board experimental MET 'Feltham' No 320 (the only one of the prototypes to survive with London Transport postwar) at Golders Green. *London's Transport Museum*

*Right:* Boarding a standard MET 'Feltham' on route 21. *London's Transport Museum*

*Above:* 'Diddler' No 43, in original LUT livery, is overtaken by a single-deck LGOC LT1059 outside Wimbledon Town Hall, 3 May 1933. *London's Transport Museum*

*Below:* In sylvan Thames-side South West London a 'Diddler' does little to disturb the peace as it heads almost silently on its way *c*1932. *London's Transport Museum*

*Above:* Vastly more modern-looking 'X1' No 61, the Chiswick-bodied prototype centre-entrance, 74-seat LUT trolleybus, heads over the now-redundant tram tracks on Kingston Bridge, June 1933. *Ian Allan Library*

why — were rather ugly, brutish-looking contrivances, although, to be fair, vastly more comfortable than the trams they replaced; which was what mattered.

The 60 'Diddlers' were merely the prelude to what would eventually become the largest trolleybus fleet in the world. The true forerunner of this fleet was No 62. Completed early in 1934, it was, like just about every aspect of 1930s London Transport design, a classic. There were similarities with the standard STL, but the markedly different livery and route indicators disguised these; in any case the former tram people based at Charlton Works retained a good deal of independence within the London Transport set-up, so the standard London trolleybus — a design which would hardly alter between 1934 and 1950 — was distinctive, elegant and original. It certainly put the advocates of retaining the tram on their back foot and finally ended any lingering hopes they might have had. No 62 seated 70 passengers in its all-metal body, which was built by Metro-Cammell. The use of established bodybuilding firms, other than London Transport itself, was a feature of the trolleybus fleet, although LPTB ensured that strict guidelines were followed, so that differences between one manufacturer and another were largely superficial.

There were in addition two further prototypes which were rather different from No 62 and did not lead to production versions, although both remained in service throughout the 1930s. No 61 was a centre-entrance six-wheeler, introduced by London United in 1932. An AEC/English Electric, it had a body built by the LGOC at Chiswick and looked extremely modern. In one sense it set the pattern for the future, for it bore little resemblance to any Chiswick bus body, being much smoother and more streamlined than contemporary STLs. The ex-tram men of the Trolleybus Department retained a good deal of independence within the LPTB set-up and always maintained an individual approach to registrations, livery, indicators, and upholstery, ignoring what the motor-bus boys were up to. No 61 was probably nearer to what a Q-type trolleybus would have looked like — one was planned but never built. No 63 was a four-wheeler with a modified standard provincial English Electric body, the only four-wheeler in the fleet.

*Right:* 'X3' No 63, London's one and only four-wheel trolleybus. *London Transport*

*Below:* 'X2' No 62, prototype for the largest and most up-to-date fleet of trolleybuses in the world, at the AEC works in Southall. In the background is a Q coach for an independent operator. *Ian Allan Library*

# • 9 •

# Trolleybuses for Trams
# — the Services

IF the introduction of the Kingston-area trolleybuses in 1931 was the prelude to the end of London's trams, the actual programme was signalled on 23 November 1933, when a parliamentary Bill to replace 80 miles of route was published by London Transport. The Act received Royal Assent nine months later, and on 27 October

1935 the work began. Two more ex-London United routes, linking Hounslow with Shepherd's Bush and Hampton Court with Hammersmith, were replaced by trolleybuses; then in November the worn-out Dartford-area trams succumbed. Early 1936 saw trolleybuses taking over the routes between Sutton and Crystal Palace via Croydon, these being combined into one through one, the 654. The replacement of the Hammersmith–Acton route in April saw only two ex-LUT services (7 and 55) still operated by trams, and even these lasted just a few

The almost-completed Bexleyheath depot in November 1935. *Ian Allan Library*

Acton depot, now home to trolleybuses but with the network of tram tracks still intact, in 1936.
*London Transport*

months longer. This was doubly ironic, for the 7 was the long and heavily used Uxbridge Road route and was home to the scarcely five-year-old 'Felthams' — trams designed with this route partly in mind. And now, in the first decade of the new millennium, there are serious proposals to reinstate trams here. But as far as the 1930s were concerned, go the trams must. West London's loss was South London's gain, for the 'Felthams' were transferred to Telford Avenue, Streatham, where the entire class would take up residence before the decade was out.

July saw the Hammersmith–Acton tram route replaced, this being followed by two ex-MET routes linking Acton and Canons Park. In some ways the MET was the most progressive of all the tram concerns taken over by London Transport, for as far back as 1925 its Manager, C. J. Spencer, who had visited Canada and the USA in 1919, was asked by Lord Ashfield to design a completely new, advanced type of tramcar. The result, after various experiments, was the 'Feltham'. Some years ahead of the LCC the

MET had put in hand a modernisation programme for its older cars, and although all of these were withdrawn for scrap by the end of 1938, there was more than a hint of the ex-LCC people at Charlton favouring their own, for the ex-LCC 'E1' was noticeably slower than its modernised ex-MET counterpart.

The MET trams between Edgware and North Finchley and between Paddington Green and Sudbury and Edgware were replaced by trolleybuses in August 1936, whilst early autumn saw inroads into the former LCC East London network serving the Docks and the edge of Epping Forest. This continued in 1937 with the replacement of the ex-Walthamstow Corporation route 85, the updated Walthamstow

*Above:* Surely the conductor of this 'E1', bound for London's oddest (and most approximate) destination on what is clearly a warm summer's day, is not trying to catch the passing breeze?
*J. Bonnell, courtesy LCC Tramways Trust*

'E1'-type trams (faster than the standard ex-LCC cars) being moved south to Telford Avenue to work alongside the 'Felthams'. That summer saw a wholesale wiping-out of East London tram routes serving the Docks and Stratford and the introduction, *inter alia*, of London Transport's highest-numbered trolleybus route, the 699 (actually the highest LPTB route number of any sort), which ran between Chingford Mount and the Victoria & Albert Docks.

In the West tram route 32, which terminated just north of Chelsea Bridge, was replaced by a revised 137 motor-bus route, whilst much further south London's longest regular trolleybus route (630) came into existence, connecting West Croydon with the quaintly named (and a constant delight to collectors of curios) 'Near Willesden Junction'. One wonders just what mayhem *Does the Team Think . . . ?* would have made of it, if only this programme — and *Mornington Crescent* — had been around at the time. There were a number of cutbacks, rather than outright withdrawals, in the Wandsworth/Battersea area, which meant that Wandsworth depot would until 1950 be home to both trolleys and trams.

Over in the mysterious East the march of the trolleybus continued with the disappearance of one of the two No 1 tram routes, together with 1A, the result being that trolleybuses far outnumbered trams on Stratford Broadway; the Wanstead Flats–Canning Town and Wanstead Flats–Upton Park routes also succumbed to the trolleybus. In February 1938 the Barking local routes were converted; then, before the month was out, the unique Alexandra Palace route was replaced by motor buses. What made it unique was that it was worked by single-deck cars — bogie vehicles built by the MET, the only examples in London. With their clerestory roofs and absence of windscreens they made a curious contrast when lined up in Wood Green depot alongside 'Feltham' cars. Up North, Waltham Cross said goodbye to trams, Edmonton becoming a trolleybus depot, although its address remained Tramway Avenue.

The year 1939 inaugurated a huge drive to remove trams from North and East London, no fewer than

*Above:* Two stylish gents, clearly in no hurry, cast a critical eye over an 'E1' on route 9 as it changes from conduit to overhead power. Trolleybus wires for replacement route 609 are already in position in this March 1938 view. *Author's collection*

23 routes being replaced by one motor-bus and 20 trolleybus routes. February saw trolleys taking over the Holborn Circus–Wood Green, London Docks–Stamford Hill and Moorgate–Stamford Hill services from seven different tram routes, whilst a month later the big, looping, much-used 53 from Tottenham Court Road to Aldgate via Stamford Hill became the 'K1'/'K2'-operated 653; 'K1s' and 'K2s' would always be associated with Stamford Hill. Summer saw trams depart from the green fastness of Epping Forest, routes 55, 55EX, 57, 57EX, 81 and 81EX being replaced.

Although World War 2 would prolong the lives of most south-of-the-Thames routes, initially its outbreak had no effect, and early in September route 77 between West India Docks and Smithfield gave way to trolleybuses, whilst in November routes 61 and 63,

linking Aldgate with Leyton and Ilford respectively, were replaced. Peace, of a sort, still reigned in the East End, this being the period of the 'Phoney War', although its inhabitants were only too aware of hostilities, for ships sailing out of the Docks — the busiest in the world — were regularly being sunk by German submarines and surface raiders such as the *Admiral Graf Spee*. The last tram-replacement scheme of 1939 saw 'J3' and 'L1' trolleybuses fitted with a special braking system plying up and down the steep hill to/from Highgate Village on route 611. The final trolleybus-for-tram replacements would occur in 1940.

What did the travelling public think of the change from trams to trolleybuses? All the evidence suggests it was delighted. They were softened up by LPTB's highly sophisticated publicity department with, under a heading 'The Street of Tomorrow', phrases such as 'the silence of smooth-running and silent new trolleybuses, successors of 30-year-old trams', and 'the new vehicle falls into line with road custom and plays its part in the evolution of the street of the future'. Traffic receipts almost always went up wherever trolleybuses replaced trams, even if they sometimes dropped back a little once the novelty of the new mode of transport had worn off.

<h1>• 10 •</h1>

<h1>Trolleybuses for Trams<br>— the Vehicles</h1>

LONDON Transport inherited 1,662 trams from the LCC, 150 from the LUT, 316 from the MET, 52 from the South Met, 40 from Ilford Corporation, 56 from East Ham Corporation, 134 from West Ham Corporation, 50 from Leyton Corporation, 54 from Croydon Corporation, 62 from Walthamstow Corporation, 33 from Bexley and 19 from Erith — a grand total of 2,628. Not all saw service with the LPTB, for some were so decrepit that they were withdrawn immediately. Many belonged to the very first generation of tramcars, the oldest dating

One of the hazards of tram travel — and one which played a significant part in its decline — is illustrated in this 1933 view of intending passengers stepping far into the road at Finsbury Park to board MET 'G'-class No 233, fitted with an LGOC-built top cover.
*London's Transport Museum*

back to the year of Queen Victoria's death. Which was one very good reason why the tram was doomed; imagine what a hoo-ha there would have been if passengers had been asked to ride around London in 1933 in a motor bus dating from 1901.

The standard tramcar was the 'E1'. This was scarcely more modern, the design dating from 1907, although examples continued to be built until 1930 — and not just by the LCC. Over the years there had been improvements, 'Pullmanisation' being the term applied, possibly by a joker within the LCC, to the fitting of upholstered 2+1 seating downstairs and upholstered cushions (but not to the backrests) upstairs. Very few of any of the cars inherited by London Transport had windscreens or vestibule screens, which was the term generally used. In other words the poor motorman had to stand, exposed to everything the weather could throw at him. Even many of

*Above:* An open-top SMET four-wheeler dating from the first decade of the 20th century stands at the top of Anerley Hill, with the magnificent (if by now somewhat careworn — and soon-to-be-burned-down) Crystal Palace dominating the scene, *c*1933. *Author's collection*

*Below:* The Embankment, along which more than 400 trams passed every hour. Heading towards Blackfriars Bridge is 'E1' No 952, whilst ahead of the windscreen-fitted 'E3' is 'E1' No 1101 working the 18A to Norbury station, the boundary between the territories of the LCC and Croydon Corporation. The photograph dates from July 1933. *Author's collection*

*Above:* Mile End Road in November 1933, with trams, including 'E1' No 912 on route 63, buses, a costermonger with barrow, pony and cart, etc. *London's Transport Museum*

*Below:* An 'E3' emerges from Kingsway Subway on its way to Highgate as a policeman bars the way to an LT on route 177, September 1933. *London Transport / Pamlin Prints*

the 'E3s' and 'HR2s' of 1930 were built in this condition. Perhaps the most extraordinary attempt to hold back progress was the purchase by Ilford Corporation in 1932 of eight brand-new open-fronted, four-wheel cars from Brush — this at a time when the MET and LUT were already operating 'Felthams'. Four-wheelers never rode as well as bogie cars, and as for specifying no windscreens in 1932, one wonders whether the genius in the corporation that made this decision didn't also ask that shafts be provided in case electric traction proved to be a passing fad and a reversion to horses proved necessary.

*Above:* An 'E1', still sporting the three colour lights (albeit now painted over) used to indicate its route in the days before World War 1, stands at a loading island, complete with shelter. *Charles F. Klapper / The Omnibus Society*

*Below:* Car No 795 and a Thomas Tilling STL pass the Catford 'Bon Marché' in 1933. A standard 'E1', No 795 was rebuilt in 1932, fitted with a metal-framed windscreen and painted aluminium and grey. By 1933 it was painted in standard livery of red and off-white livery. Despite the modifications, No 795 would be broken up by 1940. *A. D. Packer*

*Above:* Ex-MET 'G'-class No 2264 heads past the high cinema wall by the 'Tally Ho', North Finchley, on its way to Holborn, shortly before being replaced by trolleybuses in late 1938. *Photomatic*

*Right:* A postman empties a box outside an Underground station — which he might do half a dozen times a day — as three MET 'G'-class cars (the first, No 2279 with a windscreen, the other two without) pass by. *London's Transport Museum*

The LPTB decided that this really was not on, and although it very quickly took the decision to fit screens to the entire fleet, the actual fitting took very much longer and was not quite complete by the end of the decade. In the mid-1940s one of the highlights of a journey to Purley was to peer over the gates of Purley depot from the upper deck of a 'Feltham' and view what was stored out of service therein. This consisted of open-fronted 'E1s', a condition I assumed had been caused by bomb damage, but I later realised that these cars, made redundant by the final conversions of 1939/40, had never received screens and had been placed in store in case they were needed to replace cars destroyed by enemy action.

East Ham, West Ham, Walthamstow and Croydon all had variations on the 'E1' theme, whilst Leyton went one better with 50 'E3s'. All continued to operate throughout the 1930s, eventually transferring to South London depots, some lasting until the final day of trams in 1952. As the programme of replace-

ment by trolleybus rolled on through the second half of the 1930s so the tram fleet diminished.

Practically all of it was reduced to scrap, at various sites around the network, but some examples escaped and migrated north. The Ilford four-wheelers of 1932 were sold to Sunderland and, ironically, outlived the London network, lasting until 1954. They made an extraordinary contrast with another London exile, the centre-entrance 'Feltham', No 2136. This could not be equipped with plough pick-up like the rest of the 'Feltham' fleet when it was transferred to Telford Avenue, so the lucky citizens of Stockton became the beneficiaries when in 1937 it became No 100 in the Teesside fleet. Today, back in MET livery as No 331, it is the sole surviving 'Feltham' upon which one can regularly travel, at the National Tramway Museum at Crich — an experience greatly to be savoured.

Another survivor is a West Ham four-wheeler, UEC car No 102 of 1910; set aside for preservation in 1938, initially in London Transport livery, it now forms part of the LT Museum collection at Covent Garden and has been restored to West Ham livery, complete with period passengers. Three 'HR2' cars of 1930 were sold to Leeds in 1939 — a decision which the LPTB probably regretted, for the class suffered badly during the war, 16 being destroyed. Luckiest by far was No 1858. This was bought for preservation in 1952, put on static display at Chessington Zoo, where it was lucky to escape vandalism (and I don't mean by the inmates), and eventually made its way to that home for semiretired London trams and

trolleybuses, the East Anglia Transport Museum at Carlton Colville, where it has been lovingly restored to working order.

Two 'E1s' are still with us. Although withdrawal began in 1938, and more than half had been scrapped by the end of 1940, the survivors formed the most numerous type of tram in the fleet throughout the 1940s. No 1025 was saved for posterity and, preserved in the condition in which it ran in its final years, now forms part of the LT collection. A few others were sold for holiday homes on Hayling Island, and one of these, most remarkably, is once again at work at Crich. This is No 1622. What remained of it was rescued, and it was decided that, as a representative of the standard 'E1' already existed in preservation, No 1622 should be restored as one of the rehabilitated examples, of which more anon, and this is the form it now takes as it plies up and down the Pennines — a rather different setting from where it began.

A substantial section of MET No 94, a bogie car of 1904, originally double-deck but now a single-decker with a handsome clerestory roof, operates on the Seaton Tramway in Devon. Then there is LUT 109, which, like No 1622, is being put back together, some seven decades after it last ran, by those indefatigable people at the National Tramway Museum.

The LCC's pride and joy, No 1, saw little service, most drivers being wary, so the story goes, of its air brakes. It was repainted red in 1938, sent south to Telford Avenue, whence it appeared at rush hours on short workings — I never saw it come south of Thornton Heath Pond — migrated to Yorkshire along with the 'Felthams' in 1951 and eventually moved a little way southwest from Leeds to Derbyshire, where it can be seen, restored to London Transport red, as a static exhibit at Crich. It would be nice to see it running again.

London Transport took over a number of four-wheel cars and quickly got rid of all but the ex-LCC 'M' class, which looked just like shortened 'E1s'. Their riding was best described as 'lively', and despite various attempts to sober it up remained so until the class became extinct, in 1939. Three were rebuilt extensively as bogie cars. One, No 1446, did not actually re-enter service in its new form until after the London Transport takeover, whilst No 1444 (soon renumbered 1370) was rebuilt again in 1935. Both looked much more modern than anything else in the fleet, other than the 'Felthams' and Nos 1 and 2, to which they bore more than a passing resemblance, with their roller-blind indicators and domed roofs. No 2 is sometimes referred to as the only tram to be built by London Transport. It was actually an extensive rebuild of damaged 'E1' No 1370 and re-emerged modernised with fully upholstered seating and a much more up-to-date external appearance, being clearly related to No 1.

The final attempt at providing London with a modern fleet went off very much at half-cock. Knowing that it would be at least 10 years before all the trams were replaced (Herr Hitler's delaying tactics

*Above:* One of the ex-LCC 'M'-class four-wheelers drafted in by the LPTB to take over from the worn-out Corporation cars at Dartford. *London's Transport Museum*

*Right:* Wheel-carrier No 012, converted from an LCC 'L'-class car of 1909. *Author's collection*

*Far right:* Class B2 short-wheelbase trolleybus No 105 at the Woolwich terminus of route 698 on a damp day in 1936. *London's Transport Museum*

having not yet entered into the calculations), the LPTB announced in 1933 that it would 'rehabilitate' 1,000 'E1s'. This number was subsequently whittled down to 250 and then 154, and the rehabilitation proved to be very disappointing. Some, initially, did not even have windscreens, and the flat roof was retained, despite the vast improvement a domed one was seen to effect on Nos 2 and 1370. Certainly internally and externally there were improvements, and the preserved No 1622 displays these to perfection, but the 'rehabs' could hardly be described as state-of-the-art.

The trolleybus, by contrast, had achieved total modernity, No 62 setting the standard for the entire fleet, and the various 'K', 'L', 'M', 'N' and 'P' classes of 1939/40 were little different from No 62 or the 'C' types of 1935/6. The 'B1s', 'B2s' and 'B3s' of 1935/6 were a window-length shorter and had 60 seats against 70 for the rest of the fleet, being designed for the routes that scaled the heights of Highgate and Crystal Palace. It is most curious that despite

numerous variations the AEC double-deck motor bus throughout the 1930s remained classified STL, whilst the slightest change from the trolleybus norm meant a new designation, such that 'P1' had been reached by 1940.

Chassis for the trolleybus fleet were supplied by AEC and Leyland, in roughly equal quantities, but six firms built the bodies, all to the London standard but with subtle variations; these were BRCW, Brush, Weymann, Metro-Cammell, Park Royal and Leyland. Most of the earlier trolleys had spats over the rear wheels and a longitudinal seat beside the driver; this latter was soon seen to be not a good idea, and the driver was soon provided with a proper full-width, glazed bulkhead.

In 1938 there came a small but surprisingly significant change in the appearance of the standard trolleybus when 'J3' No 1054 arrived from BRCW with valances along the tops and sides of the front upper-deck windows elegantly curved into the frames, producing a distinctly streamlined effect — if not quite

*Above:* A February 1939 picture of 'K2' No 1223 being driven onto the traverser at Stamford Hill depot. *Ian Allan Library*

as dramatic as that achieved by the contemporary streamlined LNER 'A4' and LMS 'Coronation' Pacifics and Malcolm Campbell's *Bluebird* land-speed-record-holder. By contrast the Leyland 'K1' and 'K2' classes of 1938/9 — and, indeed, the 'K3s' of 1940 — refused to succumb to even the modest nod towards streamlining around the upper-deck front windows that was now standard on all other body suppliers.

Although chassis suppliers were restricted to AEC and Leyland, the 'L1', 'L2' and 'L3' classes of 1938-40 were of 'chassisless' (integral) construction with AEC running units and Metro-Cammell bodywork. They proved to be just as sturdy as vehicles with chassis, remaining in service until the very end of the system. They were for long associated with the East End, spending most of their lives, along with the contemporary Leyland 'K' classes, in East and North East London.

*Above left:* 'C1' No 182 being demonstrated to a group of trainee trolleybus drivers — presumably ex-tram men — at Fulwell depot on 26 November 1935. *London's Transport Museum*

*Left:* Unlike motor buses the trolleys nearly all had registrations that corresponded with the fleet number. 'J1' No 932 is saluted by Prince Albert as it rounds his statue at the Holborn Circus terminus of route 621 in 1938. *Ian Allan Library*

Silver was the preferred colour for the roofs of London buses and trolleybuses, but in 1938 experiments began on the latter with red, which would become standard; almost certainly this was nothing to do with the Munich crisis, when war almost arrived only to be postponed for a year, following which every shiny silver roof, be it on a motor bus or a trolleybus, would be rapidly be overpainted to make vehicles less visible to Nazi bombers.

One oddity was No 1671 (the highest number reached by 1939), a Leyland demonstrator with twin steering and a single rear axle; in other respects it was more-or-less identical to the 'K1's, 'K2s' and 'K3s'. Another oddity was 'X5' No 1379, which was designed to operate through the Kingsway Subway and had both near- and offside entrance/exits. Tests were carried out on battery power, but clearances in places were extremely tight, and, with the three subway trams routes surviving the cull of all other North London trams by 1939/40, No 1379 took up duties as an ordinary vehicle with its offside doors permanently fastened, and the idea of running trolleybuses through the Kingsway Subway was quietly dropped.

# · 11 ·

# The Underground Expands

IN some respects congestion in Central London in the 1930s was as bad as it had ever been or ever would be, and although there would be no extensions to the railways beneath its streets there were many to the suburban lines bringing passengers into the heart of the City and the West End. Thus London Transport's railway system — like so much of the Board's activities during this period —saw unparalleled expansion. Much of this involved the construction of new lines, the remainder the takeover of existing lines from the LNER, LMS or GWR.

A year before the creation of London Transport the Metropolitan Railway had opened a branch from Wembley Park to Stanmore. In 1939 this would be handed over to the Bakerloo Line, which would reach it by way of new tunnels from Baker Street to Finchley Road and then running parallel to the Metropolitan tracks. The 'Tube' trains stopped at all stations between Baker Street and Wembley Park, the surface trains became 'expresses' stopping only at Finchley Road. Staying with the Metropolitan Line, not all was expansion, for the remote rural fastness beyond Aylesbury, to Quainton Road, Brill and Verney Junction, was abandoned, the line to Brill being given up entirely in November 1935, and that to Quainton Road and Verney Junction in July 1936. Quainton Road was still served by LNER trains (and decades later would become one of the most eclectic preservation centres, with the London Underground well represented), whilst LMS trains still served Verney Junction. On the last day of December 1933 passenger trains ceased to run between Rickmansworth and Watford, although the connection remains as I write.

In September 1932 the Metropolitan District extended services over LMS tracks from Barking to Upminster. In the west the Piccadilly Line greatly extended its empire by taking over some Metropolitan District services. From October 1933 the Piccadilly assumed the Hammersmith–Ealing/Uxbridge services, extra tracks being constructed between Turnham Green and Northfields, on the

Hounslow branch. From March 1933 Piccadilly Line trains shared the route to Hounslow West with the Metropolitan District. Some splendid new Charles Holden-designed stations were erected, and the area, which at the beginning of the 1930s was still fairly rural and in character quite distinct from London, now underwent huge changes, thousands of houses, shops and all that went with suburbia appearing at a bewildering rate. This, of course, would continue after World War 2, Heathrow being chosen to replace Croydon as London's principal airport.

In October 1932, after a sustained campaign by a certain football club, the name of the Piccadilly Line station at Gillespie Road was changed to 'Arsenal (Highbury Hill)'; the result was a dramatic upsurge in attendances, this providing the ultimate vindication of the club's move some years earlier from the old Woolwich Arsenal south of the Thames (one of the advantages claimed for this having been that the new North London ground would be 'within 12 minutes' "Tube" ride of the centre of London'). Meanwhile work was proceeding apace on one of the most significant of all the Underground and 'Tube' extensions, that of the Piccadilly Line northeast from Finsbury Park.

Finsbury Park has always been an extremely busy traffic interchange, being the location of the first station on the East Coast main line out of King's Cross as well as a meeting point for trams, trolleys, Green Line coaches and motor buses, and by 1930 overcrowding on the 'Tube' was so bad that Parliament passed a Bill authorising a 7.7-mile extension of the Piccadilly Line to Cockfosters, then on the edge of the countryside. Known as the Southgate Extension, it was completed in the remarkably short time of three years, the first trains running the full length of the line on 31 July 1933. More than any other, it is an example of why London Transport was held in such high esteem throughout the world, for its eight new stations have come to represent all that was best about urban transport architecture. The consulting architects were Adams, Holden and Pearson.

*Above:* Acton Town Piccadilly Line station, typical of
Charles Holden's superb work for London Transport.
*London's Transport Museum*

*Left:* The distinctive cylindrical form of Charles Holden's
Southgate station, completed in 1933.
*London's Transport Museum*

Frank Pick and Charles Holden had toured
Northern Europe in 1930, studying the striking new
buildings there, much influenced by the Dresden
Bauhaus (which would be an early victim of Hitler)
and the work of W. M. Dudok in the Netherlands
and Gunnar Asplund in Sweden. 'Fitness for
Purpose' was the creed, and although Holden,
perhaps tongue in cheek, called his stations 'brick
boxes with concrete lids' they were superbly fitted for
their purpose, at both platform and street level
distinctive, without surplus ornamentation — a
reaction to late Victoriana and High Edwardiana —
but with a deep regard for appropriate materials.
Almost all now have listed status, and although
aspects have been modernised this has been done
with great care, and they remain essentially as
completed in the 1930s, still performing with great
efficiency, and in a sense have become timeless, a
tribute to the foresight of those remarkable men who
planned and built them.

*Above:* Art-deco interior of Cockfosters Underground station. *Author*

*Right:* Underground sign outside Southgate station. *Author*

*Below:* A recent portrait of Arnos Grove Underground station. This building, in common with many other Charles Holden designs, holds Grade II listed status. *Author*

Their fame was instantaneous. In the 1930s Nikita Khrushchev, later to become leader of the USSR and the denouncer of Josef Stalin, was in charge of the Moscow Underground (then being extended with little consideration of cost) and sent two young engineers to look at the Piccadilly Line stations. They were much impressed but on returning home were told by Khrushchev that if they were to have any chance of Stalin's approving a decadent capitalist design they needed at least to double its size — which was what they did, and the results are there today for all to see!

Amongst the many impressive statistics associated with the Southgate extension is that 12 million bricks were used (numbers of bricks used in large construction projects is always mind-blowing). Many millions more went into the estates of rather upmarket houses which sprang up along the line. That at Oakwood was described by its builders, Laing, as 'the most beautiful estate in North London'. Often they were bought by East Enders and others from inner-city areas who were moving up the social scale, in terms of both employment and general aspirations. The style of the houses was generally a good deal less adventurous than that of London Transport's stations. 'Tudorbethan', with its bay windows, stuck-on beams and leaded windows, was all the rage, although in some houses art-deco touches could be found, particularly in the metal-framed, curved windows. The developers often gave them daftly pretentious names: goodness knows what they were doing labelling their bottom-of-the-range, three-bedroom semis (costing £910) as 'Lockerbies'.

The Northern Line, as it became in August 1938 (the long-winded City & South London & Hampstead & Highgate 'Tube' had already been renamed once before, in 1934, as the Morden–Edgware Line), was much involved with taking over LNER suburban lines. The LNER had electrification plans but not the money to carry them out, and its articulated, high-capacity, low-comfort, teak-bodied suburban carriages were a byword for all that was bad about steam-hauled commuting; it is interesting to note that the carriages provided by the LNER for its most affluent commuters on the line out of Marylebone to the Chilterns were far superior. The London Transport New Works Programme of 1935-40 included the takeover by the Northern Line of the LNER branches from East Finchley to High Barnet, from Finsbury Park to Edgware (and construction of an extension thence to Bushey Heath) and from Highgate to Alexandra Palace. A good deal of construction work was carried out, and 'Tube' trains began running to East Finchley in July 1939 and to High Barnet a year later. However, a slowdown in house building, the looming war and then the war itself put paid to the other planned Northern Line extensions — just for the time being, it was supposed, but after 1945 the creation of the Green Belt, amongst other factors, meant that the curtailment became permanent. Others planned or under construction, notably the Central Line out to West Ruislip alongside the GWR main line to Birmingham to the west and to Loughton and the Roding Valley in the east, taking over from the LNER, were duly completed in the immediate postwar era.

*Above:* Alexandra Palace LNER station in 1932. The Alexandra Palace branch was intended to become part of the Underground system, but World War 2 intervened, and it never did, eventually closing in the 1950s. Class N1 0-6-2T No 4587 has charge of a train for King's Cross. *H. C. Casserley / Pamlin Prints*

*Below:* London Transport's takeover of the LNER branches north of East Finchley under the New Works Programme of 1935-40 involved considerable construction to link the new sections with existing Northern Line metals. *Ian Allan Library*

# · 12 ·

# The Ultimate
# in Commuter Trains

A train of arc-roof 'Ashbury' stock.
*Ian Allan Library*

L
ONDON Transport inherited a very mixed bag of 'Tube' and surface stock; to replace most of this it had by 1939 produced two designs, which, like so much of that to which the Board's inspired innovators turned their hands, became classics. First, though, we'll take a look at their predecessors.

On the Central Line cars dating back to Edwardian times, albeit considerably modernised, continued at work until the summer of 1939. Part of this modernisation involved replacing the original labour-intensive gates with automatic doors. The first 'Tube' trains so equipped from new entered service in 1920 on the Piccadilly Line, being transferred some 10 years later to the Bakerloo Line, where they stayed until 1939, then being withdrawn — but not broken up, in case wartime depredations required their reinstatement.

Next came what would be known as the 'Standard' stock. Six prototypes were revealed to the press at the

beginning of 1923 as 'Underground Pullman Specials' — a particularly silly title that merely debased the currency, for, although they were a commendable advance on what had gone before, no 'Tube' carriage ever has been or ever could be comparable to real Pullman comfort. Orders were then placed, initially for 191 cars. Production would continue until 1934, by which time 1,466 'Standard' carriages were in service.

There was much variation in surface stock. We'll begin on the Metropolitan. The most archaic were the 'Ashburys'. These were arc-roofed compartment vehicles dating from 1898-1900 and designed to be hauled by electric or steam locomotives. A number were converted to operate as multiple-units. Eight driving motor carriages, eight driving trailers and 41

*Above:* A seven-car Metropolitan Line train of compartment stock in original lined livery. *London Transport*

*Below:* A similar train in London Transport days in plain brown livery. The third, fourth and fifth carriages are examples of the final, steel-sided variation of the MET's compartment stock. *London Transport*

*Above:* A Circle Line train of 1913 stock.
*London Transport*

*Right:* The motorman's view ahead of a Circle Line train.
*London Transport*

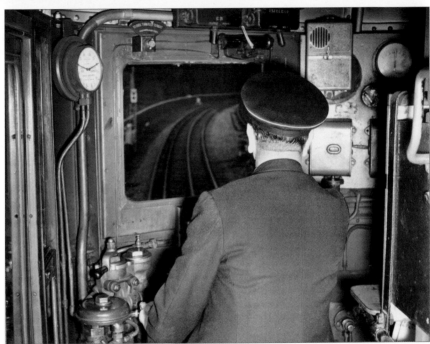

trailers passed into London Transport ownership and soldiered on until 1939. To complete the story, we must note that six were converted in 1940/1 to work as two steam-hauled push/pull units on the Chesham branch, thus ensuring the eventual preservation of several of them.

Next came the 'Dreadnoughts'. These were vastly more modern, elliptical-roof, compartment-type hauled carriages, of a design which would not have looked out of place at Glasgow Central, Carlisle, Crewe or Manchester Central, although the curved top to the doors was a distinctive feature. The first were placed in service in 1910, the last in 1923. Very similar in appearance were some compartment-type multiple-units. Twelve motor cars entered service in 1927, and 15 'Dreadnoughts' were converted to run with them; a further 55 motor cars and trailers arrived in 1930, and a final 65 in 1932.

We have noted the inappropriate use of the Pullman term for trams and 'Tube' trains, but two proper Pullmans did work on the Underground. Named *Galatea* and *Mayflower*, they were bought by the Metropolitan Railway in 1910. Their chief purpose was to provide refreshment on certain Aylesbury-line trains, which they did until 1939.

The Metropolitan Railway's saloon stock entered service over a long period, between 1904 and 1926, and its history is very complicated — not surprising, considering that there were no fewer than 535 cars in all, of which all but 13 passed into LPTB ownership. Like most long-lived Underground vehicles they were much modified and modernised. Systematic withdrawal began in 1935, but there were still plenty working the Inner Circle, as it was generally known when, as a small child, I began to travel in them in the early 1940s. As they rattled through the tunnels there was

something about their antiquated interiors that I found spookily threatening in a Grimm's Fairy Tales sort of way, and, as a consequence, for several years I refused to let my parents take me underground.

The District Railway classified its carriages built between 1905 and 1914 as 'B', 'C', 'D' and 'E' stock. 'B' stock had wooden bodies, the rest steel. Some 287 'B'-stock cars passed to the LPTB, along with a total of 112 'Cs', 'Ds' and 'Es'. Withdrawal of the 'B' stock began in 1935, but virtually all the later types continued in service throughout the 1930s. Much more modern-looking, despite their rather small oval cab windows, were the 100 all-steel 'F'-stock cars ordered in 1919. On these the clerestory roof was abandoned, and they were capable of much faster acceleration and higher speeds than their predecessors. They lasted long into postwar days.

Fifty 'G'-stock cars came next, in 1924/5. These had larger, rectangular cab windows but (rather surprisingly, perhaps) reverted to clerestory roofs. Similar, but with a smoother appearance, were the 101 'K'-stock cars of 1928/9. The final District cars to enter service before the London Transport takeover were the 37 'L'-stock cars of 1931/2. London Transport would bring this series of largely identical cars to a conclusion in 1936, when 28 'M'-stock and 26 'N'-stock vehicles took up work. Remarkably they perpetuated the tradition of clerestory roofs — a feature long considered outdated on the main line. This ensured that regular travel in a clerestory-roofed carriage could be sampled as late as the 1970s on the East London Line, where this stock ended its days — the very last clerestory-roofed carriages in ordinary service in the UK.

*Left:* A Metropolitan Line train of seven compartment carriages, hauled by one of the Bo-Bo electric locomotives, and a Bakerloo Line 'Tube' train of 'Standard' stock. *London's Transport Museum*

*Above:* A four-car train of 1932 stock destined for the Piccadilly Line poses at Lillie Bridge depot against the impressive backdrop of Whiteley's. *Ian Allan Library*

*Right:* Servicing a Piccadilly Line train of 1932 stock. *London's Transport Museum*

'Tube' trains by necessity have to be small, and not being able to use the entire space above the floor for people had always been a source of frustration to designers. By the mid-1930s advances in technology meant this was no longer the situation, so yet another icon of transport design, the 1938 'Tube' stock, was born. First of all came some fascinating but not entirely practical highly streamlined prototypes. The last of these was given a flat front and — Bingo! — perfection was achieved. Just as Holden's stations were designed without unnecessary decoration, with respect for the materials of which they were constructed and with their purpose always in mind, so it was with the 1938-stock 'Tube' trains that passed beneath and through them. The production cars first entered

*Above:* A Bakerloo Line train composed largely of 1938 stock (although the third and seventh vehicles are earlier) leaving Bushey alongside the West Coast main line. *J. C. Flemons*

*Below:* A Bakerloo Line train of 1938 stock on its way to Stanmore pauses beside at a Holden-designed station. *London Transport*

*Right:* Interior of 1938 stock. *London Transport*

service in 1938 and eventually reached the impressive total of 1,121, built by Metro-Cammell and BRCW. They served London faithfully for many decades, and even as I write in 2007 a handful are still in service, far away across the water on the Isle of Wight.

*Left:* A close-up of the elegant, flared sides of the 'Metadyne' stock. *London's Transport Museum*

*Below:* Interior of 'Metadyne' stock. *London Transport*

Equal in terms of purity of design but perhaps just that bit more revolutionary in appearance was the 1938 stock's big brother, the 'O' or 'Metadyne' stock for the District and Metropolitan lines. The two types had much in common, with flush-fitting windows, excellent use of internal space and fine detailing. But the one big variation was that the surface stock had flared-out sides. This was said to be to stop the dangerous practice of passengers' leaping onto footboards at the last minute and being carried off into the tunnel hanging onto the handrails. However, one wonders if this really was a serious consideration and suspects that, just like the flared-out fronts of the streamlined 'Tube' stock, this was more a matter of styling, very much in tune with the times. Initially there were 116 cars made up into two-car sets, but variations soon appeared, a trailer being added to each set. Then came the 'P' stock for the Metropolitan Line, which began work in July 1939. Thirdly came the 'Q' stock, which was designed to work with older stock. The grand total of all three variations was 573.

The future is now. The high-point of high-capacity, urban railway design. 'Metadyne' surface and 1938-stock 'Tube' trains north of Neasden. *London's Transport Museum*

• 13 •

# War

London Transport had prepared itself well for the war that by 1938 just about everyone knew was inevitable. War was declared on 3 September 1939 and, in anticipation of immediate deadly bomber raids on London, an evacuation plan that had been finalised at a meeting held five months earlier at the Ministry of Transport was put into effect. Provision had been made for approximately 1,218,000 people to be moved to safer areas, 609,000 of these being schoolchildren and their teachers, the others 'children under school age with their mothers, escorts, blind persons and expectant mothers'.

The evacuation was carried out within four days — a quite remarkable achievement. The effect on many of the children, removed with sometimes not even the opportunity to say goodbye, was also remarkable — and highly distressing. Some 1,280 motor buses and 670 trams and trolleybuses were used to take the people to '129 entraining stations' away from the main-line termini (to avoid too much congestion) to Ealing Broadway, Acton, Burnham

(Bucks), Sudbury Hill, Harrow, Edgware, Enfield West, Bounds Green, Richmond, Wimbledon and New Cross Gate, amongst others. Use was also made of Underground trains where these connected with main-line stations. The plan stipulated that the vehicles used were to be 'taken off their normal services at the times they are required to make the special journeys' and would 'return to their normal services as soon as they have completed the conveyance of the evacuation traffic'.

Various measures were immediately put into effect in early September, although a strange, halfway state existed with no raids on England — although elsewhere, particularly at sea, hostilities began at once. Services were cut, leading to the withdrawal of hundreds of buses, particularly those with limited capacity, such as all the remaining Dennis Darts, as well as double-deckers — practically all the Tilling STs, many of the General version and the forward-entrance Country Area STLs. These all eventually returned to service, the Tilling STs in particular being

*Left:* A policeman warns of an air raid as the drivers of ST212 and an unidentified STL hurry to take cover on the day World War 2 broke out, 3 September 1939. The primitive use of pedal-cycle and whistle was a relic of World War 1; vastly more sophisticated methods — chiefly sirens, which could be heard over a long distance — would be in place by the time the bombs began to rain down on London a year later. *London's Transport Museum*

*Right:* A smiling nurse emerges from a 10T10 Green Line coach converted to an ambulance and engaged in evacuating patients and staff from Westminster Hospital, 1 September 1939. *London's Transport Museum*

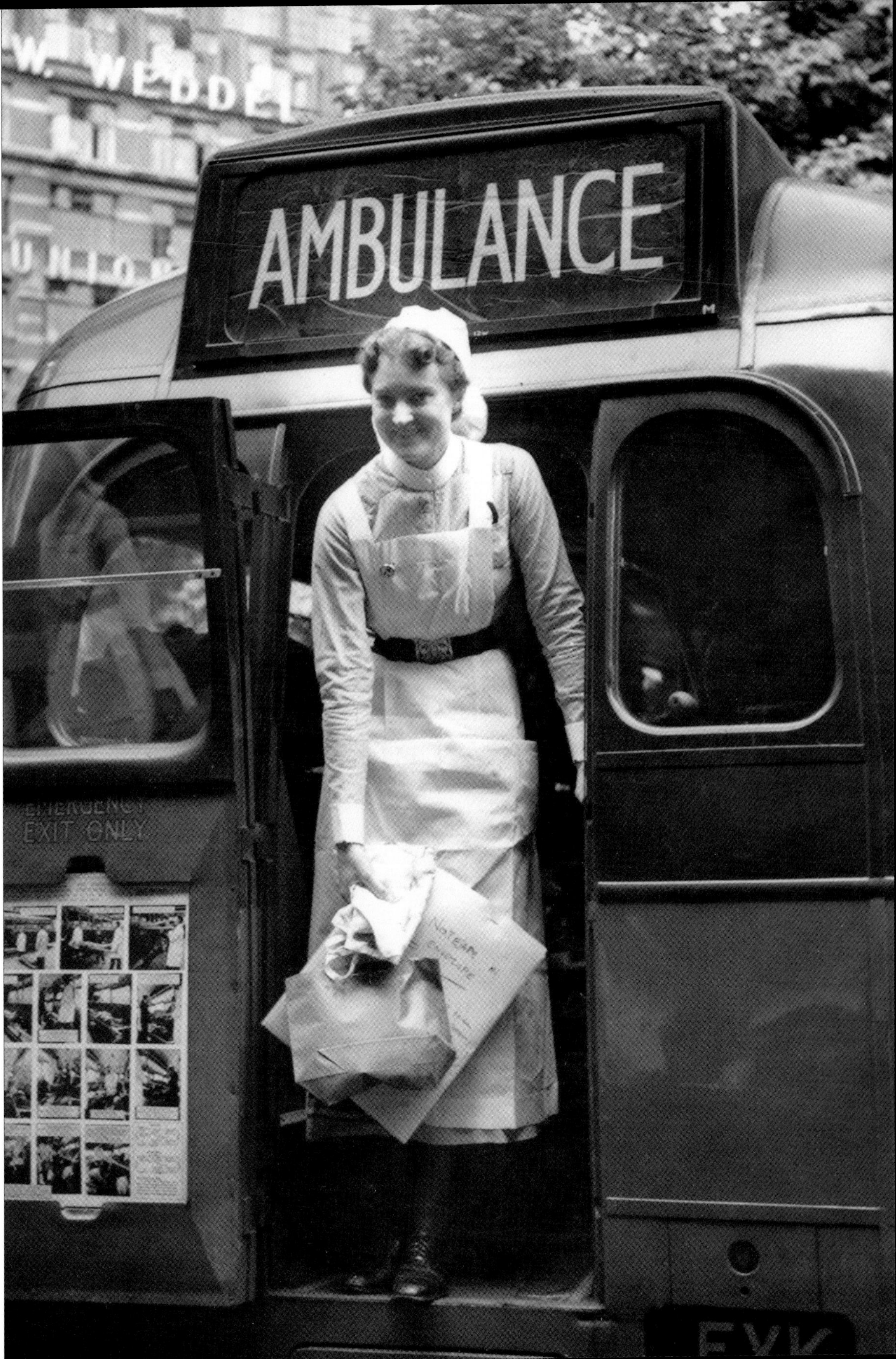
AMBULANCE
EMERGENCY
EXIT ONLY

sent to help out all over Britain. The entire Green Line network disappeared, most of its coaches being converted into ambulances, although it was later, temporarily, partially reinstated, being worked by double-deck buses.

Probably the most noticeable change on the home front was the imposition of the Blackout, with reduced interior lighting on all trains, buses, trams and trolleys, and masked headlights. The result was many accidents, some fatal. Manufacturers of white paint prospered, for platform and mudguard edges, tram fenders and boarding platforms were all painted white in an attempt to make them more visible.

The Dunkirk evacuation and the fall of France in June 1940 was succeeded by the intense bombing campaign on London so long anticipated. It was because so much had been achieved by London Transport in the previous decade that its buses, trams, trolleybuses and Underground trains — and, above all, the men and women who controlled and operated them — were able to keep the capital moving through those dreadful times and emerged, battered and worn but triumphant, when victory was finally achieved. But that, as they say, is another story.

Girls from the Charles Edward Brooke School board three 'E3' tram cars in Camberwell New Road on their way to Waterloo station to be evacuated by train, 1 September 1939. *London's Transport Museum*

*Above:* Early experiments with producer gas involved this Country Area ST, seen having its gas trailer filled with anthracite at Chiswick Works on 16 November 1939. *London's Transport Museum*

*Below:* The Officer's Mess cook of the 84th (London Transport) Anti-aircraft Regiment, Territorial Army, giving instructions to two members of the Women's Auxiliary Territorial Service at a training camp in Bude, Cornwall, 7 August 1939. *London's Transport Museum*

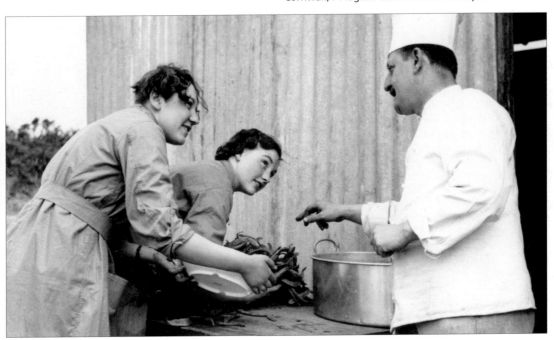

An unbroken line of contemporary London buses
personifies the London of the 1930s in this view recorded
at Victoria Station towards the end of the decade. Present
are Chiswick-built STL and ST classes of AEC Regent and an
LT Class Renown. With the onset of World War 2
London Transport would have to 'make do and mend'
with these existing types and place a moratorium on the
development of future models. *Ian Allan Library*

# Bibliography

*Bare Empty Sheds* by G. Harry Guilmartin
(Tramway & Light Railway Society, 1986)
*LCC Electric Tramways* by Robert J. Harley
(Capital Transport, 2002)
*Green Line* by Laurie Akehurst and David Stewart
(Capital Transport, 2005)
*Labour Relations in London Transport* by H. A. Clegg
(Augustus M. Kelley, 1950)
*The Last Years of the General* by Ken Glazier
(Capital Transport, 1995)
*A Lifetime of Bus Work* by Robert Scanlan
(Transport Publishing Co, 1979)
*London Bus File, Double-deckers 1933-39*
by Ken Glazier (Capital Transport, 2001)
*London Bus File, Single-deckers 1933-39*
by Ken Glazier (Capital Transport, 2002)
*London Buses Before the War* by Ken Glazier
(Capital Transport, 1996)

*London Transport Tramways Handbook*
by D. W. Willoughby and E. R. Oakley
(published by the authors, 1972)
*The London Trolleybus, Volume 1* by Ken Blacker
(Capital Publishing, 2002)
*London's Underground*, ninth edition, by John Glover
(Ian Allan Publishing, 1999)
*London's Underground Suburbs* by Dennis Edwards
and Ron Pigram (Baton Transport, 1986)
*The Metropolitan Electric Tramways, Volume 2*
by C. S. Smeeton (Light Rail Transit Association,
1986)
*The STLs* by Ken Blacker (Capital Transport, 1984)
*Steam to Silver* by J. Graeme Bruce
(Capital Transport, 1983)

Various issues of *Passenger Transport*

Various documents in London's Transport Museum